Preface

Getting Started with Windows® 10 and Microsoft® Edge uses a simple, visual approach to teach the necessary skills for using the Windows 10 operating system and Microsoft Edge web browser, plus OneDrive and OneNote. It also introduces the Office apps, tools for creating screenshots, and the Snip & Sketch app. This brief program will help you gain the proficiency needed to open and use applications, navigate between and within applications, manage files, get information from the internet, and share files and information on a PC with Windows 10 installed. In addition, it will help you master basic skills for customizing and maintaining the Windows operating system.

Courseware Based on Office for the Web and Office 365 Features

Both Microsoft Office for the web and Microsoft 365 are continually updated. Specific features and functionality of Microsoft 365 applications vary depending on the user's account, computer setup, and other factors. This edition of the *Getting Started with Windows® 10 and Microsoft® Edge* courseware was developed using features available as of May 2020. You may find that with your computer and version of Office for the web or Microsoft 365, the appearance of the software and the steps needed to complete an activity vary slightly from what is presented in the courseware.

Course Features

The following guide shows how this instructional content uses a visual, step-by-step, competency-based approach to teach the basic skills you need to use a PC running Windows 10 successfully at home, school, or work. Clear and concise text and screen captures teach essential concepts, features, and skills in an easy-to-understand format.

A **chapter overview** describes the topics you will cover in the chapter.

A **Skills You Learn** list itemizes the tasks you will be able to accomplish at the end of the chapter.

A **Files You Use** section lists the student data files you will need to complete the skills in the chapter. Some chapters will not use data files.

Getting Started with

Windows 10

and Microsoft® Edge

2020 Edition

plus
OneDrive™
Office for the web
OneNote®
File management
Internet browsing
Screen capturing

Faithe Wempen
Indiana University – Purdue University Indianapolis
Indianapolis, IN

Lisa A. Bucki
Co-Founder of 1x1 Media, LLC
Leicester, NC

PARADIGM
EDUCATION SOLUTIONS

Minneapolis

Vice President of Content Management: Christine Hurney
Director of Production: Timothy W. Larson
Production Editor: Emily Tope
Cover Designer, Senior Design and Production Specialist: Julie Johnston
Tester: Denise Seguin
Indexer: Beverlee Day, Guided by Words Indexing Services
Digital Projects Manager: Tom Modl
Supervisor of Digital Products and Onboarding: Ryan Isdahl
Vice President of Marketing: Lara Weber McLellan
Marketing and Communications Manager: Selena Hicks

Care has been taken to verify the accuracy of information presented in this book. However, the authors, editors, and publisher cannot accept responsibility for web, email, newsgroup, or chat room subject matter or content, or for consequences from the application of the information in this book, and make no warranty, expressed or implied, with respect to its content.

Trademarks: Microsoft is a trademark or registered trademark of Microsoft Corporation in the US and/or other countries. Some of the product names and company names included in this book have been used for identification purposes only and may be trademarks or registered trade names of their respective manufacturers and sellers. The authors, editors, and publisher disclaim any affiliation, association, or connection with, or sponsorship or endorsement by, such owners.

Paradigm Education Solutions is independent from Microsoft Corporation and not affiliated with Microsoft in any manner.

Cover Illustration Credit: © OtreeStudio/Shutterstock.com
Interior Image Credits: *Page ix*, © Oleksiy Mark/Shutterstock.com; *page x*, (top, left to right) © Sambrogio/iStock.com, Courtesy of Sandisk Corporation, © Gmnicholas/iStock.com; *page xi*, (top) © IhorL/Shutterstock.com, (bottom) © Nomad_Soul/Shutterstock.com; *pages 41–42*, Google and the Google logo are registered trademarks of Google Inc., used with permission; all screen captures of Microsoft products are used with permission from Microsoft.

We have made every effort to trace the ownership of all copyrighted material and to secure permission from copyright holders. In the event of any question arising as to the use of any material, we will be pleased to make the necessary corrections in future printings.

ISBN 978-1-7924-3653-6

© 2020 Paradigm Education Solutions
7900 Xerxes Avenue S STE 310
Minneapolis, MN 55431-1118

Email: CustomerService@ParadigmEducation.com
Website: ParadigmEducation.com

Contents

A **skill introduction** describes the features and tasks you will explore in the skill.

Numbered steps and screen captures provide instant reinforcement to help you learn each skill quickly and easily.

Tip features offer hints and troubleshooting advice.

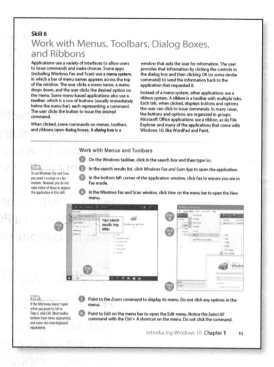

Another Way features provide alternative methods for performing steps, including keyboard shortcuts.

Skill Extras offer additional information about the topics covered in a skill.

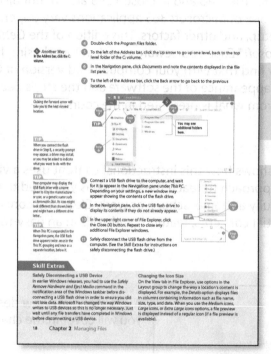

A **Tasks Summary** lists the key tasks covered in the chapter, along with the ribbon commands used to initiate them as well as shortcuts and alternative ways to perform them.

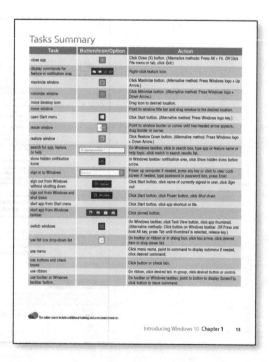

The Cirrus Solution
Elevating student success and instructor efficiency

Powered by Paradigm, Cirrus is the next-generation learning solution for developing skills in Microsoft Office and Microsoft 365. Cirrus seamlessly delivers complete course content in a cloud-based learning environment that puts students on the fast-track to success. Students can access their content from any device anywhere, through a live internet connection. Cirrus is platform independent, ensuring that students get the same learning experience whether they are using PCs, Macs, or Chromebook computers.

Cirrus provides access to all the *Getting Started with Windows® 10 and Microsoft® Edge* content, delivered in a series of scheduled assignments that report to a grade book to track student progress and achievement. Assignments are grouped in modules, providing many options for customizing instruction.

Dynamic Training
The Cirrus *Getting Started with Windows® 10 and Microsoft® Edge* courseware includes interactive resources to support learning.

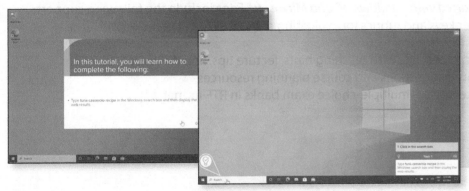

Guide and Practice Tutorials lead students through the steps to complete each skill and then allow students to practice on their own. These tutorials include simple instructions and optional help.

Student Data Files needed to complete the course activities, review exercises, and assessments may be downloaded as a zipped file from the Course Resources section of the online course and are also provided within Cirrus activities as needed.

Online Extras expand on the topics covered in the chapter activities. Read these brief summaries to discover additional features and functionality.

Review and Assessment
Review and assessment activities in the Cirrus environment offer multiple opportunities to reinforce learning, apply skills, and check mastery.

A **Knowledge Check** presents 10 multiple-choice questions on key concepts and features.

Skills Review exercises offer practice completing the skills.

Skills Application exercises provide more challenging practice, combining actions in a different order and applying them in a slightly different context, with less direction.

Skills Assessment offers an opportunity to apply skills in an engaging, real-world scenario without step-by-step guidance. Each assessment includes an image showing how the student's screen should look.

Concepts Exams use multiple-choice questions to assess understanding of key features and skills.

Student eBook

The Student eBook makes *Getting Started with Windows® 10 and Microsoft® Edge* content available from any device (desktop, laptop, tablet, or smartphone) anywhere. The eBook is accessed through the Cirrus online course.

Instructor eResources

In addition to these Cirrus-specific tools, other instructor materials are available. Accessed through Cirrus and visible only to instructors, the Instructor eResources for *Getting Started with Windows® 10 and Microsoft® Edge* include the following support:

- Answer keys and rubrics for evaluating responses to chapter exercises and assessments
- Lesson blueprints with teaching hints, lecture tips, and discussion questions
- Syllabus suggestions and course planning resources
- Chapter-based, multiple-choice exam banks in RTF format

Getting Started

Microsoft Windows 10 is the latest version of Windows, the most popular operating system in the world for personal computers. This courseware teaches you how to use Windows 10 with the May 2020 Update installed to accomplish basic tasks on a personal computer, such as running programs and managing files, as well as how to customize and maintain the Windows operating system. It also introduces the Microsoft Edge browser and shows you how to find information on the internet.

In addition, this courseware covers Microsoft applications designed to optimize your use of a computer running Windows 10 May 2020 Update in a personal, work, or academic environment. You will learn how to access OneDrive, a secure online storage location, and how to use Office apps. You will also learn how to take screenshots and how to collect, organize, and share research data using OneNote.

Student Data Files and Resources

This courseware includes online quizzes, student data files, interactive tutorials, Online Extras, end-of-chapter review and assessment materials, and other student resources that support the text. To complete this course, you will need access to the Cirrus courseware plus a computer that has an internet connection and the Windows 10 operating system with the Microsoft Edge browser.

The student data files you will need to complete some of the skills, exercises, and assessments are accessed from the online version of this course. Chapter 2 teaches you how to download the student data files from the online course to a USB flash drive, and Chapter 4 teaches you how to upload the student data files from the USB flash drive to your OneDrive account. You do not need student data files for Chapter 1.

Hardware and Software Requirements

This courseware is designed for a computer running a standard installation of Microsoft Windows 10 Home or Microsoft Windows 10 Pro, with May 2020 Update, on a desktop or laptop PC.

Certain chapters and skills in this courseware also assume that you have the following additional features:

- Internet access (for downloading the student data files, sending email, and using online apps)
- A USB flash drive (for storing student data files)
- A printer
- **Optional:** Speakers or headphones, and a microphone (for communicating with Cortana)

Note that Windows 10 will update over time. For that reason, you may see color and other discrepancies between the screen captures in this courseware and the interface on your computer screen.

Starting Up and Shutting Down

If you are using a computer in a school lab environment, you might not need to start it up or shut it down, because many labs leave their computers on throughout the day, turning them off only at night. If you are using your own computer, though, you will want to know how to turn it on and off.

- **To turn on the computer:** On the computer, press the power button, which loads the Windows 10 operating system. A sign-in prompt appears when Windows has finished loading. To sign in, see Chapter 1, Skill 1.
- **To turn off the computer:** On the Windows taskbar, click the Start button, click *Power*, and then click the *Shut Down* option. Shutting down in this way also signs you out. To sign out without shutting down, see Chapter 1, Skill 1.

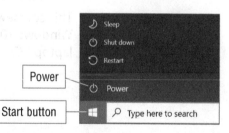

Using a Pointing Device

A mouse is a pointing device, which means it controls an on-screen pointer that you use to select text and graphics. The appearance of the on-screen pointer changes depending on what you are doing, but usually it is a small white arrow.

Here are some basic skills to master with a mouse:

- **Point:** To move the mouse so that the on-screen pointer hovers over a specific object, such as an icon.
- **Click:** To press and release the left mouse button once. Clicking usually selects the object you are pointing at. You might click a file in a file listing to select it, for example.
- **Double-click:** To press and release the left mouse button twice quickly in succession. Double-clicking usually activates the object you are pointing at. For example, if you are pointing at an icon for an application, the application runs.

left mouse button

right mouse button

scroll wheel

- **Right-click:** To press and release the right mouse button once. Right-clicking an on-screen object usually opens a menu with commands related to the object you are pointing at.
- **Drag:** To press and hold the left mouse button and then move the mouse, which takes the object with it as it moves. The primary reason for dragging is to move or resize an object.
- **Right-drag:** To press and hold the right mouse button and move the mouse. It is like regular dragging, but when you release the mouse button, a menu appears that you can use to specify what you want to happen. For example, when you right-drag a file, the menu's choices include moving, copying, and creating a shortcut to the file.
- **Scroll:** To rotate the mouse's center wheel to scroll the content in the active window up or down, as a shortcut for using the scroll bars in the window to change the view of the content. Not every mouse has a wheel.

A touchpad is a touch-sensitive rectangular pad on many laptops that can be used as a pointing device. Drag your finger across it to move the pointer. Tap the touchpad to click; double-tap to double-click. Some touchpads have adjacent buttons that work the same as the right and left buttons on a mouse.

This courseware assumes you are working on a desktop or laptop PC, and instructions refer to the keyboard and mouse as the primary input devices. However, if you have a touchscreen, you may use it for input in most cases. Note that touchscreens function differently than a mouse or touchpad, and you will need some special skills to use this form of device. Here are a few important terms you should know:

Tap (or touch). Tap the screen with one finger, pressing and quickly releasing on the same spot. You tap to make a selection or issue a command.

Stretch (or unpinch). Touch two fingers to the screen in adjacent spots and then drag the fingers farther apart. You stretch to zoom in (and display a smaller area).

Pinch. Touch two fingers to the screen in different spots and then drag the fingers together. You pinch to zoom out (and display a larger area).

Drag (or slide or swipe). Touch one finger to the screen and then slide it along the surface. You drag to perform a variety of functions, depending on the software and context. For example, dragging can open menu bars, exit applications, scroll the display, or move items around on the screen.

Rotate. Touch two fingers on the desired object or area and then drag them in a circular motion.

Using a USB Flash Drive

A flash drive is a small personal storage device. You will need a flash drive to store and work with the files needed to complete the skills in this course.

A flash drive connects to a Universal Serial Bus (USB) port on a personal computer. Nearly all Windows 10 computers have multiple USB ports. Some USB ports have higher maximum transfer speeds than others, but any will work for your flash drive for this course.

To connect a USB flash drive, press its connector gently but firmly straight into an empty USB port on the PC. It only fits in one direction, so if the connector doesn't go in easily, try turning the drive over.

Creating an Account on a Windows PC

In a school or work setting, you will probably be assigned a user name and password to use when signing in to Windows 10. The user name may be an email address. If you already have a user name and password, there is no need to create another one to use with this course.

If you do not already have a user name and password, you will need to create a new user account. To do this, you must first be signed in to Windows 10 using an account with Administrator privileges and connected to the internet. You must also either have an existing email address or be prepared to create one during the process. Ask your instructor for help if needed. After you have signed in to the computer using the Administrator account, complete the following steps.

1 On the Windows taskbar, click the Start button and then click *Settings*.

2 In the Settings app, click *Accounts*.

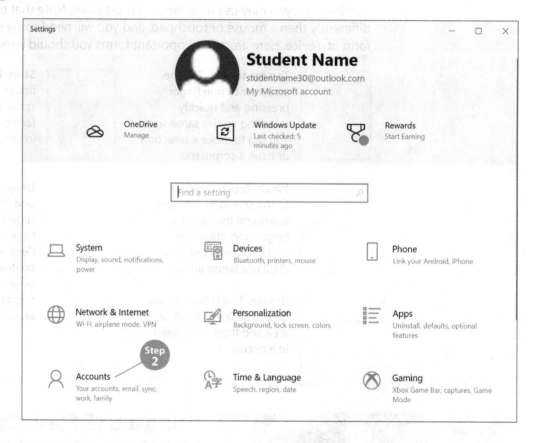

3 In the Navigation pane of the Accounts section, click *Family & other users*.

4 In the right pane, click *Add someone else to this PC*.

5 Follow the prompts that appear, filling in information as requested, to create the account. The prompts you see depend on whether you are creating a new email address or using an existing one, and whether the email address you are using has previously been registered with Microsoft.

6 Click the Close (X) button to close the Settings window when finished.

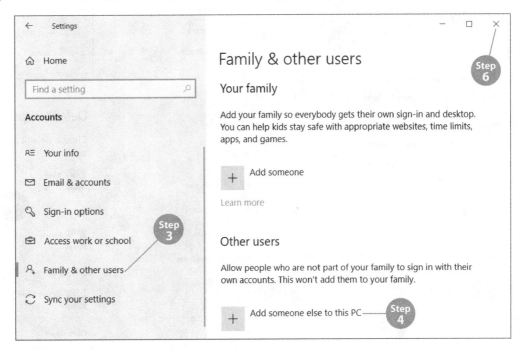

After you create the account, you may be asked to verify the account, either by responding to an email message or entering a code you get in a text message. Follow the prompts to do so. The account shown in the examples in this course was created using default settings.

Setting a Default Email Application

A few of the skills in this course involve sending email messages. This process is simple if you have a default email application configured in Windows 10, because Windows 10 opens the application automatically and starts a new email. All you have to do is fill in the recipient and the subject.

When you install Microsoft Office or Microsoft 365, its email application Microsoft Outlook may set itself as the default application for handling email. Outlook is a good choice for the skills in this course because it works seamlessly with most other Windows applications. However, you can also choose to make a different email application the default if you wish. Your choice of application must be a real application, and not just a web interface for web-based email such as Yahoo! Mail, Gmail, or Outlook.com.

To set your default email application, follow these steps:

1 On the Windows taskbar, click in the search box and then type default.

2 In the search results list, click *Default apps System settings*.

3 In the Default apps window, click the link for the current email app.

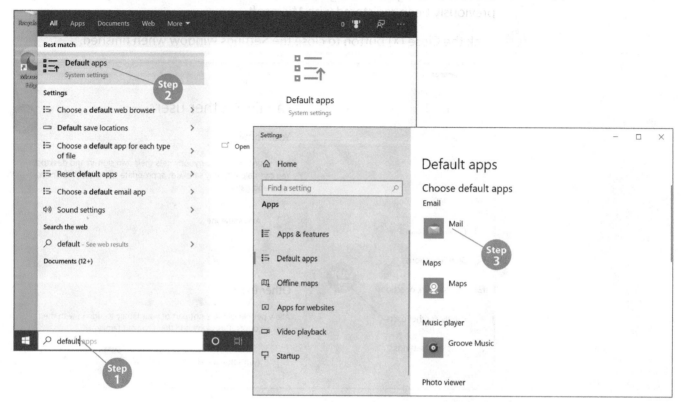

4 In the *Choose an app* list, click the desired application.

5 Click the Close (X) button to close the Settings window.

Chapter **1**

The online course includes additional training and assessment resources.

Introducing Windows 10

Windows 10 is an operating system for personal computers. An *operating system* creates the user interface that you interact with, runs programs, manages files, and connects to networks. Windows 10 runs on many different computer types, including desktop PCs, laptop PCs, and tablets.

The Windows environment is based on movable rectangular areas called *windows*. Almost everything happens within a window, including running applications, browsing the web, and working with files. In this chapter, you will learn to navigate the Windows 10 interface and how to open, close, and manipulate these windows. You will also learn how to use some standardized controls within a window, such as menus, toolbars, ribbons, and dialog boxes.

Skills You Learn

1 Sign In to and Out of Windows 10

2 Explore the Windows 10 Desktop, Taskbar, and Start Menu

3 Open and Close Applications

4 Manipulate Windows

5 Move between Open Windows

6 Work with Menus, Toolbars, Dialog Boxes, and Ribbons

7 Get Help in Windows

Files You Use

For these skills, you do not need any student data files.

Sign In to and Out of Windows 10

To use Windows, you must *sign in*. Signing in usually involves selecting a user account and then typing a password. Depending on how your school's PCs are configured, you may already have been assigned a user name and password with which to sign in to Windows PCs. If so, use them in the following steps. If not, ask your instructor what user name and password to use.

When you finish your Windows session, you should *sign out*. Signing out shuts down any running applications and data files and disconnects from any user-specific resources, such as your personal folders. If nobody will be using the computer for a while, you can also *shut down* as you sign out. Shutting down exits Windows entirely and turns off the computer's power.

TIP

The Lock screen appears when nobody is signed in to Windows or when the signed-in user has locked the PC.

TIP

In Step 4, if you are not prompted for your user name and do not see it in the lower left corner of the screen, click *Other user* to display the prompt.

TIP

In Step 4, if you click your user name in the lower left corner but do not see a password prompt, click <u>Sign-in options</u> and then click the Microsoft account password icon.

TIP

After Step 6, if this is the first time you are signing in on this PC with this account, you may be prompted to complete the account setup process. Follow the prompts.

7-9 *Another Way*
Right-click the Start button, point to *Shut down or sign out*, and then click *Sign out*.

TIP

In Step 8, if you have configured a picture for your user account, the picture appears instead of the plain icon.

1. Power up the PC, if it is not already on.

2. If you see the Windows desktop, someone is already signed in to the PC and you need to sign out. (See Steps 7–9.)

3. If you see the Lock screen (displaying a full-screen graphic with the time and date), press any key or click anywhere on the screen to open the Sign-in screen.

4. If you are prompted for your user name, type it. Or, if you see your user name in the bottom left corner of the screen, click it.

5. In the password text box, type the password for your account.

6. Press Enter or click the Submit button to display the desktop.

7. Click the Start button.

8. On the Start menu, click the User Account icon.

9. On the menu, click *Sign out* to sign out of Windows without shutting down your computer.

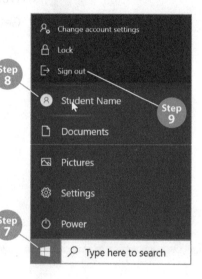

Signing Out of Windows and Shutting Down
Sometimes you might want to turn off the computer completely, not just sign out. To do so, click the Start button, click the Power icon on the Start menu, and then click *Shut down*. Alternatively, click *Sleep* to place the computer in a low-power state without shutting it down.

Explore the Windows 10 Desktop, Taskbar, and Start Menu

This skill describes the basic components of the Windows 10 interface: the desktop, the Windows taskbar, and the Start menu.

Desktop

The **desktop** is the main Windows screen that you see after you sign in. As you open windows, the windows appear on top of the desktop.

An **icon** is a small picture representing a file, folder, or program. By default there are two icons on the desktop: Recycle Bin (covered in Chapter 2) and Microsoft Edge. However, you may see others on your desktop. Some icons are shortcuts. A **shortcut** is a pointer to a file or folder located elsewhere. For example, when some applications install, they create shortcuts on the desktop so you can run them more easily.

Windows Taskbar

The **Windows taskbar** is the bar across the bottom of the desktop. At the far left end is the **Start button**. Clicking the Start button opens the **Start menu**, which is a gateway to running installed applications and accessing system settings and utilities.

To the right of the Start button is a **search box**, which provides access to the Search feature. Searching is covered in Chapter 3.

The Windows taskbar can hold pinned buttons for easy access to commonly used applications. A **pinned button**

is a shortcut that stays where it is pinned. The default pinned shortcuts on the Windows taskbar include Talk to Cortana (covered in Chapter 3), Task View, Microsoft Edge (covered in Chapter 3), File Explorer (covered in Chapter 2), Microsoft Store, and Mail. You can also pin your own favorite applications there. (See the Online Extras at the end of this skill.)

The Windows taskbar also displays a button for each open window. You can switch to an open window by clicking its button there. A button for an open window looks very much like a pinned shortcut, except that it has a colored line under it.

At the right side of the Windows taskbar is the **notification area**. It contains icons that represent programs and utilities that are running in the background. You can right-click any of these icons to see a menu for managing it. At the far right end of the Windows taskbar is a clock and an Action Center icon (for opening a pane showing alerts).

Start Menu

Clicking the Start button opens the Start menu. The Start menu contains shortcuts to many commonly used applications and utilities. Some of the shortcuts on the Start menu appear as **tiles** (colored rectangles). The main function of the Start menu is to open applications, which is covered in Skill 4.

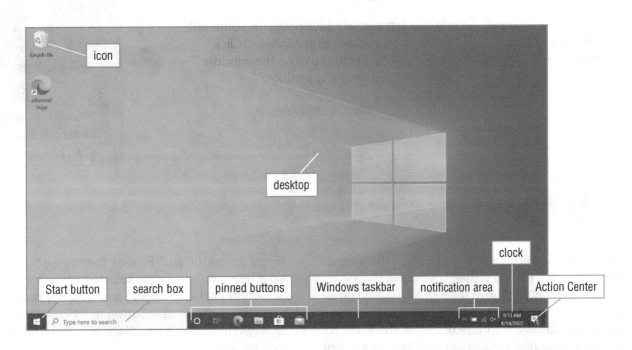

1 If needed, sign in to Windows to display the desktop.

2 Drag the Recycle Bin icon to the upper right corner of the desktop.

3 Drag the Recycle Bin icon back to its original location.

TIP

Dragging is covered in the Skill Extra at the end of these steps.

4 Point to the yellow folder button pinned to the Windows taskbar and read the ScreenTip that displays its name: *File Explorer*.

TIP

In Step 4, if File Explorer is open, you will see a thumbnail image of the window rather than a ScreenTip.

5 Repeat Step 4 to see the names of all the other pinned buttons on the Windows taskbar.

6 In the notification area, point to the icon that looks like a speaker and read the ScreenTip that displays the current speaker volume level.

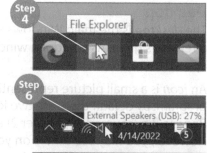

TIP

If you do not see a speaker icon, perform Steps 6 and 9 on another icon in the notification area.

7 Click the Show hidden icons button to display a list of other notification area items.

8 Click away from the list to close it without making a selection.

TIP

The icons you see in the notification area will vary depending on what applications and utilities are running in the background and what kind of hardware the PC has.

9 Right-click the speaker icon to display a shortcut menu of speaker options.

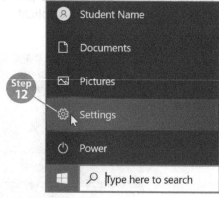

10 *Another Way*
Press the Esc key.

10 Click away from the menu to close it without making a selection.

11 *Another Way*
Press the Windows logo key.

11 Click the Start button and then move the mouse pointer up to the button with three bars so that the icons' names appear.

12 Click Settings.

TIP

Customizing Windows is covered in Chapter 6.

13 In the Settings window, notice the different options for customizing Windows. Click the Close (X) button to close the window without changing any settings.

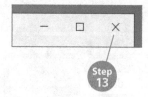

Skill Extra

Dragging

To drag an icon with the mouse, position the mouse pointer over the item and then hold down the left mouse button as you move the mouse. To drag on a touchscreen, touch and hold the item and then move your finger across the surface of the touchscreen. To drag on a touchpad, double-tap and then move your finger across the pad. Release the mouse button or lift your finger to release the selected item. Dragging is sometimes called *dragging and dropping* because when you release the mouse button or lift your finger, the dragged item drops into place wherever the mouse pointer was.

Skill 3
Open and Close Applications

An *application* (or *app*) is software that performs some useful task, such as writing a letter, sending email, or looking up information online. Windows comes with a variety of simple applications, and you can also acquire others.

Some applications have shortcut tiles pinned to the Start menu. These applications are easy to open; just click the tile. If you want to open an application that does not have a pinned tile on the Start menu, you can browse the list of installed applications that appears on the left side of the Start menu and choose it from there. You can also click in the search box, start typing the name of the application, and then choose the application in the search results list.

Open and Close Applications from the Start Menu

1 Click the Start button.

2 Click the Photos tile.

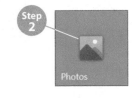
Step 2

3 Explore the Photos app by clicking the buttons along the top.

4 Click the Close (X) button to close the Photos window.

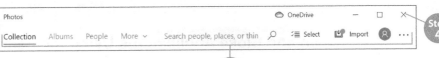

Step 3

Step 4

TIP
After Step 2, if this is the first time you've used the Photos app, a help screen may appear. Click the Close (X) button in its upper right corner to bypass it.

4 *Another Way*
Press Alt + F4 to close almost any window.

5 Click the Start button.

6 Point to the right of the list of applications so that a scroll bar appears and then drag the scroll box downward until you see the *W* section.

7 Click *Windows Accessories* to expand that category.

8 Click *Paint*. You might need to scroll down to find *Paint* on the list.

TIP
The Paint application is useful for drawing pictures and making simple edits to photos.

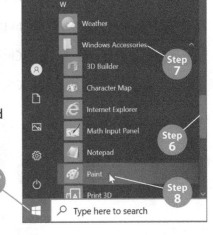

Step 5

Step 6

Step 7

Step 8

9-10 Another Way
Click the Close (X) button to close the Paint window.

9 In the Paint window, click the File tab.

10 Click *Exit* to close the Paint window.

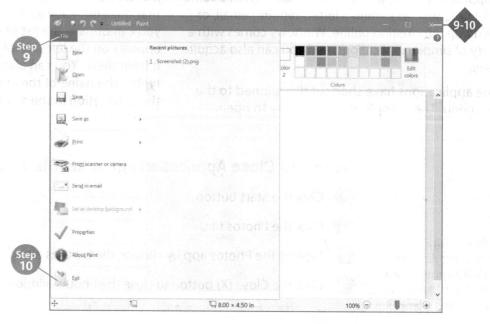

Open and Close Applications Using the Search Box

TIP

The first time you use the search box, you might see a different prompt, and you might be asked a few questions. Respond to these before continuing.

11 On the Windows taskbar, click in the search box and then type note.

12 In the search results list, click *Notepad App*.

13 In the Notepad window, type your name.

14 Click the Close (X) button to close the Notepad window.

15 Click the Don't Save button in the prompt asking if you want to save your work.

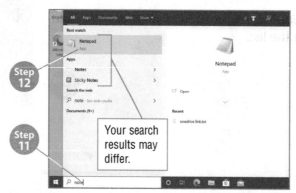

Your search results may differ.

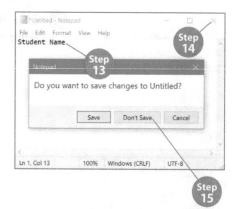

Skill Extra

Understanding Desktop and Microsoft Store Apps

Two types of applications run in Windows 10: desktop applications and Microsoft Store apps. A **desktop application** is designed to run on full-size desktop and laptop computers. Desktop applications have existed for decades. Examples include Notepad, Paint, and all the Microsoft 365 applications. A **Microsoft Store app** (sometimes called a **Universal app** or a **Modern app**) is designed to run only on Windows 8 and higher. The

Photos app you opened in this skill is an example. This type of application is typically simpler and uses less memory to run because it is created to run on any Windows 10 device, including tablets. Windows 10 S Mode, a Windows mode that is enabled by default on Microsoft Surface laptops and some other small laptops, runs only Microsoft Store apps.

Skill 4
Manipulate Windows

A *window* is a well-defined rectangular area onscreen in which an application runs, a file listing appears, or a message is displayed. As you saw in Skill 3, each application opens in its own window.

A window can appear in one of three states:

- *Maximized:* enlarged to fill the entire screen
- *Minimized:* open but temporarily hidden from view

- *Restored:* neither minimized nor maximized, and therefore able to be moved and resized

You can move and resize a window to meet the needs of the task you are performing. For example, if you have many windows open at once and you want to see all of them at a glance, you can make each window relatively small and arrange them side by side.

---

1 On the Windows taskbar, click the File Explorer button to open the File Explorer application.

 2 **Another Way**
Press Windows logo + Up Arrow.

2 In the File Explorer window, click the Maximize button if the window is not already maximized. The window enlarges to fill the entire screen and the Maximize button changes to a Restore Down button.

TIP
If you are not signed into OneDrive, a reminder to sign in appears above the *Frequent folders* list.

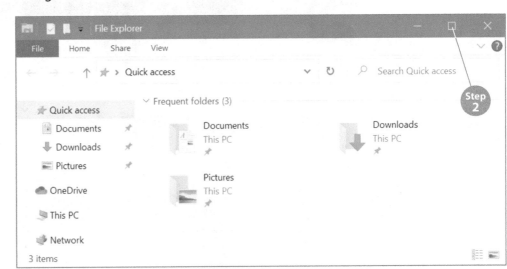

3·4 **Another Way**
Press Windows logo + Down Arrow.

3 Click the Restore Down button. The window returns to its pre-maximized size and position and the Restore Down button changes back to a Maximize button.

4 Click the Minimize button. The window disappears but the app is still running.

TIP
A colored line under a button on the Windows taskbar indicates the application is open.

5 On the Windows taskbar, click the File Explorer button. The File Explorer window returns to its pre-minimized state and position.

6 Point to the right border of the File Explorer window. The mouse pointer becomes a right-and-left-pointing arrow.

7 Drag the border to the right to enlarge the window horizontally.

Step 6

TIP

Not all windows can be resized. Some applications have a fixed window size set by the programmers who created them.

8 Point to the lower right corner of the window. The mouse pointer becomes a diagonal two-headed arrow.

9 Drag the border down and to the left to make the window taller and narrower.

Step 8

10 Point to the title bar at the top of the window. The mouse pointer does not change in this case.

11 Press and hold down the left mouse button to drag the window to a different location on the desktop and then release the mouse button.

12 *Another Way*
Press Alt + F4.

12 Click the Close (X) button to close the File Explorer window.

Step 12

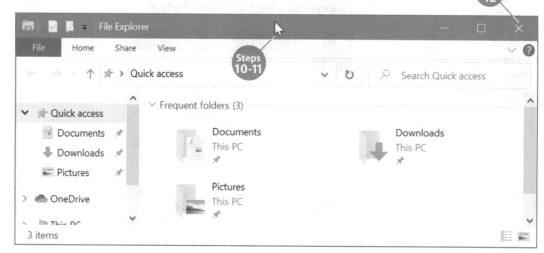

Steps 10-11

Skill Extras

Minimizing All Open Windows
Minimize all windows at once by clicking the Show Desktop button, which is the thin vertical bar to the right of the clock and the Action Center icon on the Windows taskbar, or by pressing Windows logo + M.

Using the Keyboard to Move and Resize Windows
Right-click the title bar on a window or press Alt + Spacebar, to see a shortcut menu with *Restore*, *Move*, *Size*, *Minimize*, *Maximize*, and *Close* options. In a non-maximized window, after clicking *Move* (or pressing the Down Arrow key until *Move* is highlighted), move the window using the arrow keys. Similarly, after clicking *Size*, change the window's dimensions using the arrow keys. Press the Enter key when done moving or sizing.

Snapping Apps and Automatically Maximizing Windows
If you drag an app window to the far right or left, so it is at least halfway off the screen, and then drop it there, the window is resized and positioned to cover the right or left half of the screen. This is called snapping an app. If you drag a window up so its title bar touches the top of the screen, and then drop it there, the window is automatically maximized.

Closing a Minimized Window
To close a minimized window without restoring it first, right-click its icon on the Windows taskbar and then click *Close window*.

Skill 5
Move between Open Windows

When multiple windows are open at once, you will likely want to switch between them. This is called *multitasking*. There are many different ways of moving between windows. By experimenting with the various methods, you can find the one you like best.

TIP

If the items in Steps 1–3 do not appear on your Windows taskbar, click any three buttons or icons of your choice.

1 On the Windows taskbar, click the Microsoft Edge button to open the Microsoft Edge web browser. Restore the window down if it is maximized.

2 On the Windows taskbar, click the File Explorer button to open the File Explorer window. Restore the window down if it is maximized.

3 In the notification area of the Windows taskbar, right-click the speaker icon and then click *Open Sound settings* to open the sound settings.

TIP

How to move and resize windows was covered in Skill 4.

TIP

To move a maximized window, you must first restore it down by clicking its Restore Down button.

4 If necessary, move and resize the three open windows to arrange them so that at least a portion of each window is visible.

5 On the Windows taskbar, click the Settings button to switch to that window and make it active if needed.

6 Click any visible portion of the File Explorer window to switch to that window, thus moving it to the front.

7 Press the Alt key and hold it down while you press the Tab key repeatedly. You see a screen containing a thumbnail of each open window, with the currently selected window outlined.

8 Press the Tab key until the Microsoft Edge thumbnail is selected and then release the Alt key. The Microsoft Edge window becomes active.

9 On the Windows taskbar, click the Task View button. Thumbnail images of the open windows appear, similar to those in Steps 7–8, except these stay visible without you having to hold down any keys.

10 Click the File Explorer thumbnail to make the File Explorer window active.

TIP

You can use the vertical scroll bar in Task view to scroll down for quick access to files and applications you have recently used. This feature is called *Timeline*.

11 Press Alt + Esc to make a different window active.

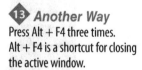
Another Way
Press Alt + F4 three times. Alt + F4 is a shortcut for closing the active window.

12 Press Alt + Esc until File Explorer is once again active.

13 Click the Close (X) button on each open window to close the three open windows.

Skill Extra

Working with Multiple Desktops

When you have many windows open at once, your desktop can get cluttered. If you want to start with a fresh-looking desktop without closing the open windows, you can create a new desktop. To do this, click the Task View button on the Windows taskbar and then click the New desktop button in the upper left corner on the desktop. Click the new desktop's thumbnail at the top of the screen (probably Desktop 2) to switch to it. To switch back to the original desktop, click the Task View button again and then click the thumbnail of the original desktop (probably named Desktop 1).

Skill 6

Work with Menus, Toolbars, Dialog Boxes, and Ribbons

Applications use a variety of interfaces to allow users to issue commands and make choices. Some apps (including Windows Fax and Scan) use a *menu system*, in which a bar of menu names appears across the top of the window. The user clicks a menu name, a menu drops down, and the user clicks the desired option on the menu. Some menu-based applications also use a *toolbar*, which is a row of buttons (usually immediately below the menu bar), each representing a command. The user clicks the button to issue the desired command.

When clicked, some commands on menus, toolbars, and ribbons open dialog boxes. A *dialog box* is a

window that asks the user for information. The user provides that information by clicking the controls in the dialog box and then clicking OK (or some similar command) to send the information back to the application that requested it.

Instead of a menu system, other applications use a ribbon system. A *ribbon* is a toolbar with multiple tabs. Each tab, when clicked, displays buttons and options the user can click to issue commands. In many cases, the buttons and options are organized in groups. Microsoft Office applications use a ribbon, as do File Explorer and many of the applications that come with Windows 10, like WordPad and Paint.

Work with Menus and Toolbars

1 On the Windows taskbar, click in the search box and then type fax.

2 In the search results list, click *Windows Fax and Scan App* to open the application.

3 In the bottom left corner of the application window, click *Fax* to ensure you are in Fax mode.

4 In the Windows Fax and Scan window, click *View* on the menu bar to open the View menu.

5 Point to the *Zoom* command to display its menu. Do not click any options in the menu.

TIP

To use Windows Fax and Scan, you need a scanner or a fax modem. However, you do not need either of those to explore the application in this skill.

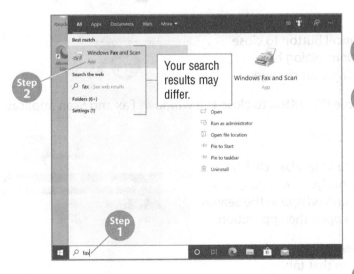

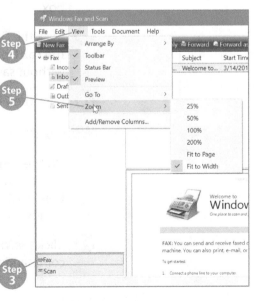

TIP

If the Edit menu doesn't open when you point to *Edit* in Step 6, click *Edit*.

6 Point to *Edit* on the menu bar to open the Edit menu. Notice the *Select All* command with the Ctrl + A shortcut on the menu. Do not click the command.

⑦ Press the Esc key to close the menu and then press the Esc key again to deselect *Edit* on the menu bar.

⑧ Point to the New Fax button on the toolbar so that a ScreenTip appears showing an explanation of the command. Do not click the button.

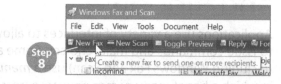

Work with Dialog Boxes

⑨ On the menu bar, click *Tools*.

⑩ On the menu that appears, click *Options*.

⑪ In the Fax Options dialog box, click the Receipts tab.

⑫ Click the *E-mail To* option button to select it.

⑬ Click the *Attach a copy of the sent fax* check box to insert a check mark.

⑭ Click the Compose tab.

⑮ Click the Font settings button to open the Font dialog box.

⑯ Click the *Color* box arrow to open the color palette.

⑰ Click the *Red* option.

⑱ Click OK to close the Font dialog box.

⑲ Click the Cancel button to close the Fax Options dialog box without saving your changes.

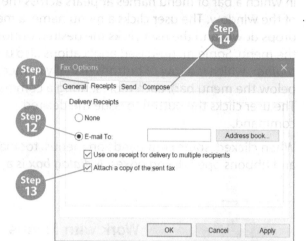

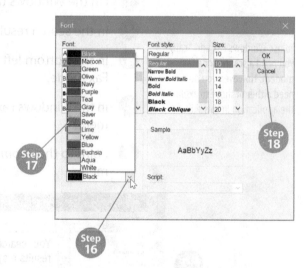

⑳ Click the Close (X) button to close the Windows Fax and Scan application.

Work with Ribbons

㉑ On the Windows taskbar, click in the search box, type wordpad, and then click *WordPad App* in the search results list to open the application.

㉒ Click the View tab to see the commands on that tab.

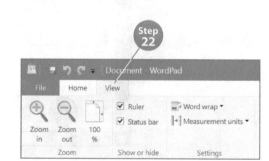

TIP

In Step 10, if *Options* is not on the Tools menu, close the menu and then click *Fax* in the bottom left corner of the application window to switch to Fax mode. (See Step 3.)

TIP

Check boxes are used for on/off settings. Unlike *option buttons*, they are independent, meaning that selecting one does not deselect another.

TIP

A drop-down list displays a menu of choices, such as colors, fonts, or sizes.

23 Click the Home tab to see the commands on that tab.

24 Point to the Align text left button in the Paragraph group to display its ScreenTip and then click the button to select it, if it is not already selected.

25 Click the Center button to select it. Notice that the Align text left button is no longer selected.

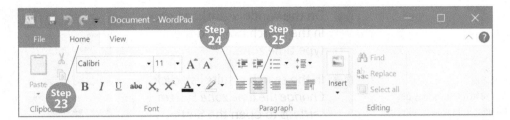

26 Click the File tab. The File tab is different from the other tabs; rather than displaying choices on the ribbon, it opens a menu.

27 Point to *Save as* and review the options on the submenu that opens. Do not click any of the options.

28 Click *Exit* to close WordPad. If prompted to save changes, click the Don't Save button.

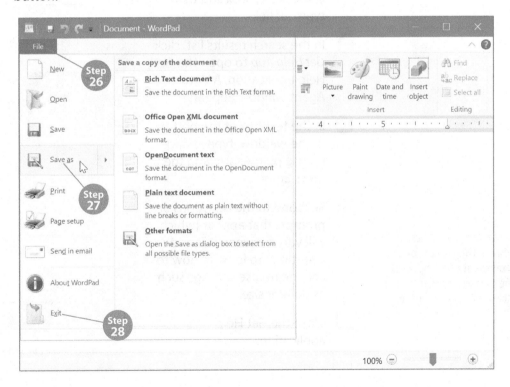

Skill Extra

Using Contextual Tabs on a Ribbon

Certain ribbon tabs appear only when something triggers them in the application, such as when a certain kind of content is selected. This type of tab is called a *contextual tab*. For example, in File Explorer, when you have selected a picture file, the Manage Picture Tools tab is available. If you are following steps that ask you to select a particular ribbon tab that you don't see, check to make sure you have selected the object that would make that tab appear.

Get Help in Windows

You can search for Windows help information using the search box on the taskbar. You can also use the Get Help application to consult the Virtual Agent. The

Virtual Agent enables you to ask questions in natural language, rather than searching by keywords.

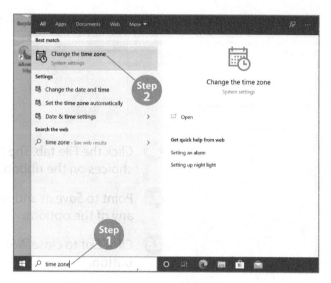

1. On the Windows taskbar, click in the search box and then type time zone.

2. In the search results list, click *Change the time zone System settings* to open the Settings app.

TIP

Your search results may be different from what is shown in the Step 2 screen capture.

3. Click the Close (X) button to close the Settings app without changing any settings.

4. On the Windows taskbar, click in the search box and then type get help.

5. In the search results list, click *Get Help App* to open the Get Help application. A Virtual Agent window appears.

6. In the text box at the bottom of the window, type change mouse pointer size and then press Enter.

TIP

In Step 7, you might click a *Change mouse settings - Windows Help* option, for example. The Get Help app is frequently updated, though, so the wording you see may differ.

7. Respond to the questions or prompts that appear (which will vary between PCs and over time) to look up how to change mouse settings such as pointer size.

8. Close the Get Help application.

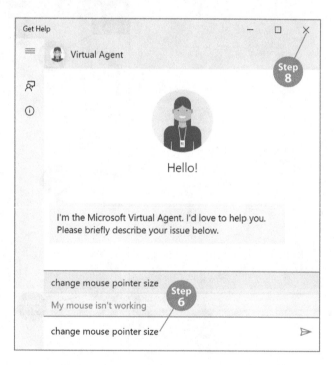

Skill Extra

Troubleshooting Network Problems

If you ever have a problem with your network connection, here's an easy and direct way to start the network troubleshooter. Right-click the networking icon in the notification area of the Windows taskbar and then click *Troubleshoot problems* in the shortcut menu.

Tasks Summary

Task	Button/Icon/Option	Action
close app	[X]	Click Close (X) button. (Alternative methods: Press Alt + F4. *OR* Click File menu or tab, click *Exit*.)
display commands for feature in notification area	[icons]	Right-click feature icon.
maximize window	[□]	Click Maximize button. (Alternative method: Press Windows logo + Up Arrow.)
minimize window	[—]	Click Minimize button. (Alternative method: Press Windows logo + Down Arrow.)
move desktop icon		Drag icon to desired location.
move window		Point to window title bar and drag window to the desired location.
open Start menu	[⊞]	Click Start button. (Alternative method: Press Windows logo key.)
resize window	[↔]	Point to window border or corner until two-headed arrow appears, drag border or corner.
restore window	[❐]	Click Restore Down button. (Alternative method: Press Windows logo + Down Arrow.)
search for app, feature, or help	[🔍 Type here to search]	On Windows taskbar, click in search box, type app or feature name or help topic, click match in search results list.
show hidden notification icons	[∧]	In Windows taskbar notification area, click Show hidden icons button arrow.
sign in to Windows	[Password →]	Power up computer if needed, press any key or click to clear Lock screen if needed, type password in password box, press Enter.
sign out from Windows without shutting down	[↦ Sign out]	Click Start button, click name of currently signed-in user, click *Sign out*.
sign out from Windows and shut down	[⏻ Shut down]	Click Start button, click Power button, click *Shut down*.
start app from Start menu		Click Start button, click app shortcut or tile.
start app from Windows taskbar	[icons]	Click pinned button.
switch windows	[⊟]	On Windows taskbar, click Task View button, click app thumbnail. (Alternative methods: Click button on Windows taskbar. *OR* Press and hold Alt key, press Tab until thumbnail is selected, release key.)
use list box drop-down list	[∨]	On toolbar or ribbon or in dialog box, click box arrow, click desired item in drop-down list.
use menu		Click menu name, point to command to display submenu if needed, click desired command.
use buttons and check boxes		Click button or check box.
use ribbon		On ribbon, click desired tab. In group, click desired button or control.
use toolbar or Windows taskbar button		On toolbar or Windows taskbar, point to button to display ScreenTip, click button to issue command.

Chapter 2

The online course includes additional training and assessment resources.

Managing Files

In this chapter, you will learn how to use the Windows 10's File Explorer utility to locate files and perform common operations on them such as moving, copying, renaming, and deleting.

A *file* is a collection of data stored under a single name, such as *MyLetter.docx*. Most files have an *extension*, which is a period followed by a few letters or numbers. In the file name *MyLetter.docx*, *.docx* is the extension. The file extension tells Windows how to handle the file. Windows maintains a list of file name extensions and which application handles them. For example, the *.docx* extension is assigned to Microsoft Word.

Files are stored locally on *volumes*. A volume is a storage location with a letter assigned to it, such as *C* or *D*. It might be a disk drive such as a hard disk, a removable disc such as a DVD, or a USB flash drive. Files can also be stored online, such as in a cloud service like OneDrive.

Within a volume, files are organized into logical groupings called *folders*. Folders typically have names that signal the purpose of the files stored within them, such as *Program Files*, *Users*, or *Downloads*. You can easily view different folders and browse their content in File Explorer, and search multiple folders for a specific file.

Sometimes groups of files are compressed into an archive file, which usually has a *.zip* extension. An archive file looks like one single file, and can be worked with as a single file, but it actually contains multiple files. It can be unpacked (decompressed) to extract the individual files within it. The data files for this textbook will come to you in a compressed archive, for example. You can also create your own compressed archives.

The *File Explorer* interface in Windows 10 makes it easy to select multiple files and then issue a command that affects all of them. For example, you can copy a group of files from your local hard drive to a USB flash drive to share with a friend. You can also delete files. A deleted file is not destroyed immediately; it is moved to the *Recycle Bin*. You can retrieve deleted files from the Recycle Bin if you change your mind about deleting them.

Skills You Learn

1 Navigate between Local Volumes and Folders in File Explorer
2 Control the Display of Hidden Files and File Name Extensions
3 Create and Rename a File or Folder
4 Download and Extract Student Data Files
5 Select Multiple Files and Folders
6 Create a Compressed Archive (ZIP) File
7 Move and Copy Files
8 Delete Files and Use the Recycle Bin
9 Search for a File

Files You Use

In this chapter you will download to a USB flash drive the data files you need for this and future chapters.

Skill 1

Navigate between Local Volumes and Folders in File Explorer

File Explorer enables you to browse all the volumes and folders connected to your PC. These storage locations might include your PC's main hard disk drive, additional hard disk drives, optical discs such as CDs and DVDs, and USB flash drives. You can browse a volume's folders to find the file you want, or you can use shortcuts provided by Windows to browse specific locations such as Documents or Pictures.

The File Explorer window consists of two panes. On the left is the *Navigation pane*, containing shortcuts to make various locations active. On the right is the file list pane, showing the contents of whatever location is active. Across the top of the window is the *Address bar*, which reports the path of the active location—for example, This PC > Local Disk (C:).

Most people store most of their data files in one of the user folders that Windows 10 provides. On a Windows 10 computer, each user account has its own separate set of user folders, so each user's work remains private when multiple people share a computer. The shortcuts to locations such as Downloads, Pictures, and Music all point to the folders for the account of the user who is currently signed in. If a different user signs in, those shortcuts point to the corresponding folders for that different user.

The *Quick access list* displays by default at the top of the Navigation pane when you open File Explorer. It contains pinned shortcuts to user folders, and also shortcuts to recently used folders.

---

① **Another Way**
Right-click the Start button and then click *File Explorer*.

① On the Windows taskbar, click the File Explorer button.

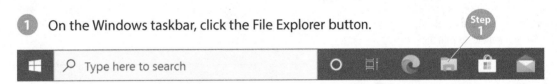

② In the Navigation pane, scroll down if needed and then click *This PC* to select it. If you see a right arrow in front of it, click the arrow to expand the listing.

③ **Another Way**
In the Navigation pane, click the C: volume. You may need to scroll down to see it.

③ In the file list pane, scroll down if needed and then double-click the C: volume.

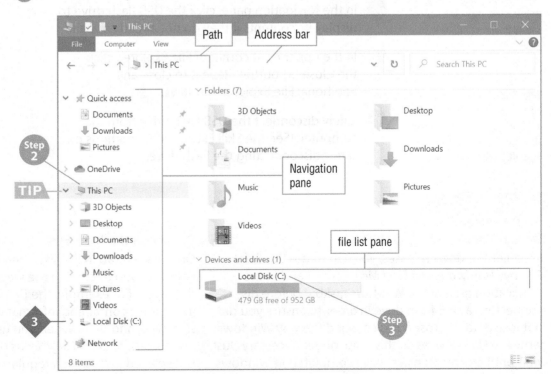

TIP

When a list is expanded, the arrow in front of it points down.

TIP

If there is no volume label assigned to a volume, it appears as Local Disk (C:). On some systems, a volume label is assigned to some disks, so you might see a different name.

④ Double-click the *Program Files* folder.

⑤ **Another Way**
In the Address bar, click the C: volume.

⑤ To the left of the Address bar, click the Up arrow to go up one level, back to the top level folder of the C: volume.

⑥ In the Navigation pane, click *Documents* and note the contents displayed in the file list pane.

⑦ To the left of the Address bar, click the Back arrow to go back to the previous location.

TIP

Clicking the Forward arrow will take you to the next viewed location.

TIP

When you connect the flash drive in Step 8, a security prompt may appear, a driver may install, or you may be asked to indicate what you want to do with the drive.

TIP

Your computer may display the USB flash drive with a name given to it by the manufacturer or user, or a generic name such as *Removable Disk*. Its icon might look different than shown here and might have a different drive letter.

TIP

When This PC is expanded in the Navigation pane, the USB flash drive appears twice: once in the This PC grouping and once as a separate location, below it.

Local Disk (C:)
File Home Share View

Step 7 ← → ∨ ↑ 💻 › This PC › Local Disk (C:) Step 4 ∨ ↻ 🔍 Search Local Disk (C:)

☁ OneDrive Step 5
💻 This PC
📁 3D Objects
🖥 Desktop
📄 Documents Step 6
⬇ Downloads
🎵 Music
🖼 Pictures
🎬 Videos
💽 Local Disk (C:)

📁 Program Files
📁 Program Files (x86)
📁 Users
📁 Windows

You may see additional folders here.

4 items   1 item selected

⑧ Connect a USB flash drive to the computer, and wait for it to appear in the Navigation pane under *This PC*. Depending on your settings, a new window may appear showing the contents of the flash drive.

⑨ In the Navigation pane, click the USB flash drive to display its contents if they do not already appear.

⑩ In the upper right corner of File Explorer, click the Close (X) button. Repeat to close any additional File Explorer windows.

⑪ Safely disconnect the USB flash drive from the computer. (See the Skill Extras for instructions on safely disconnecting the flash drive.)

∨ 💻 This PC
  › 📁 3D Objects
  › 🖥 Desktop
  › 📄 Documents
  › ⬇ Downloads
  › 🎵 Music
  › 🖼 Pictures
  › 🎬 Videos
  › 💽 Local Disk (C:)
  💾 USB Drive (D:) **TIP** Step 9
  💾 USB Drive (D:)

— ☐ ✕ Step 10

🔍 Search USB Drive (D:)

Skill Extras

Safely Disconnecting a USB Device

In earlier Windows releases, you had to use the *Safely Remove Hardware and Eject Media* command in the notification area of the Windows taskbar before disconnecting a USB flash drive in order to ensure you did not lose data. Microsoft has changed the way Windows writes to USB devices so this is no longer necessary. Just wait until any file transfers have completed in Windows before disconnecting a USB device.

Changing the Icon Size

On the View tab in File Explorer, use options in the Layout group to change the way a location's content is displayed. For example, the *Details* option displays files in columns containing information such as file name, size, type, and date. When you use the *Medium icons*, *Large icons*, or *Extra Large icons* options, a file preview is displayed instead of a regular icon (if a file preview is available).

Skill 2
Control the Display of Hidden Files and File Name Extensions

In Windows, any file or folder can be marked as hidden. By default, File Explorer does not include hidden files and folders in listings, because presumably they are hidden for a good reason, such as to protect them. However, you may need to access hidden files or folders to make system changes. For example, you may need to access the AppData folder in your user account folder to modify themes or templates for an Office application. Windows allows you to change the default setting to show files and folders that are marked as hidden.

Each file name ends with a file name extension (usually three or four characters) that indicates the file type.

For example, *.exe* indicates an executable program file and *.txt* indicates a plain text file. By default, in File Explorer listings, Windows hides the extensions for file types that are registered in its database of extensions and their assigned programs. When you are selecting files in File Explorer, you might want to see the extensions to better understand which files you are choosing. For example, if you had files named mortgage.txt and mortgage.xlsx, and extensions were hidden, those two files would both appear as *mortgage* in the file listing. They would have different icons, but they would appear to have the same name.

Show/Hide Hidden Files

1. On the Windows taskbar, click the File Explorer button.

2. In the Navigation pane, click *This PC*.

◆ **3** *Another Way*
In the Navigation pane, double-click the C: volume under *This PC*.

TIP
If the File Explorer window's ribbon is displayed on your PC, your screen will look slightly different than shown here.

3. In the file list pane, double-click the C: volume.

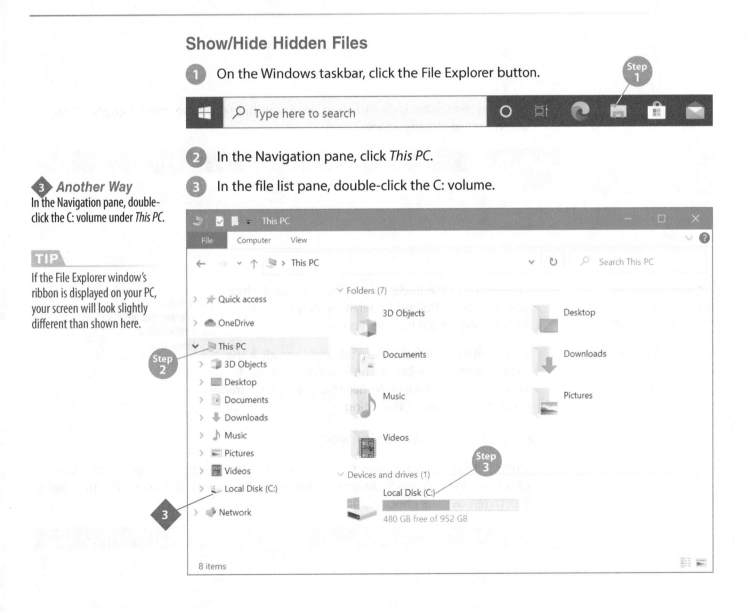

4. Double-click the *Users* folder in the file list pane. The content of that folder appears, with a folder for each user account on your PC. Make a note of the folders you see.

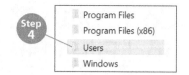

Step 4

5. On the ribbon, click the View tab.

TIP

The folders you see in the Users folder correspond to the user accounts on the local PC. Depending on who uses your computer, you will have different account folders. Do not delete any of these folders, even if you don't recognize the user names.

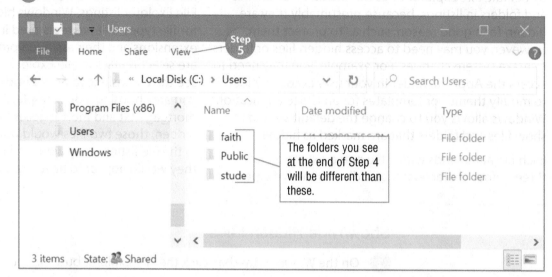

The folders you see at the end of Step 4 will be different than these.

6. Click the *Hidden items* check box in the Show/hide group to insert a check mark, if one does not already appear.

TIP

By default, none of the three check boxes in the Show/hide group contains a check mark. However, these settings may have been changed on your PC.

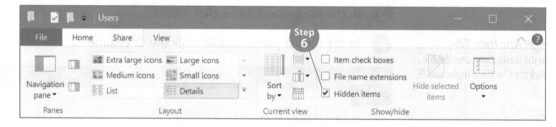

TIP

The File Explorer ribbon is collapsed by default. If you would like it to stay visible, follow the instructions in the Skill Extras at the end of these steps.

7. Look again at the folders in the Users folder listing. Now you see a Default folder. Its icon is slightly faded, indicating it is a hidden folder.

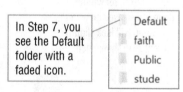

In Step 7, you see the Default folder with a faded icon.

8. On the ribbon, click the View tab and then click the *Hidden items* check box in the Show/hide group to remove the check mark. Notice that the Default folder no longer appears in the listing.

Show/Hide File Name Extensions

9. On the ribbon, click the View tab and then look to see if the *File name extensions* check box in the Show/hide group contains a check mark. If it does, click the check box to remove the check mark.

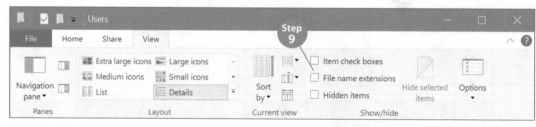

TIP
If the Address bar is obscured by
the ribbon in Step 10, press Esc
to hide the ribbon.

10 In the Address bar, click the C: volume.

11 In the file list pane, double-click the *Windows* folder.

12 In the vertical scroll bar for the file list pane, drag the scroll box all the way down
to the bottom. Extensions are hidden for files with known types, so very few
extensions appear.

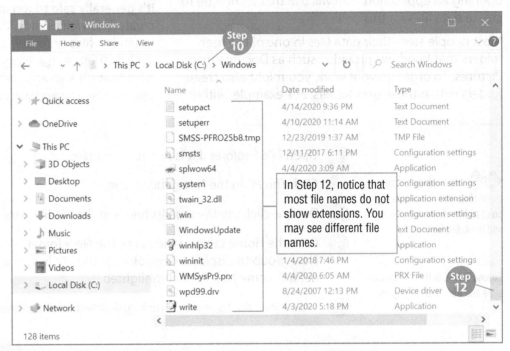

In Step 12, notice that most file names do not show extensions. You may see different file names.

TIP
By default, Windows displays
only the file extensions for which
it does not have an associated
application.

13 On the ribbon, click the View tab and
then click the *File name extensions*
check box in the Show/hide group to
insert a check mark. Drag the vertical
scroll bar all the way down again.
Notice that almost all the file names
now show extensions.

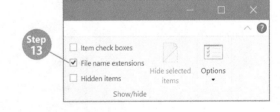

14 Click the View tab and then click the *File name extensions* check box to remove
the check mark. If either of the other two check boxes are marked, click those
check boxes to remove those check marks as well. Leave File Explorer open for
the next skill.

Skill Extras

Keeping the Ribbon On All the Time
In File Explorer, depending on your settings, the ribbon
might appear only after you click one of its tabs. You
can set the ribbon to stay on all the time. Start by
clicking one of the tabs to view the ribbon, and then
click the pushpin at the far right of the ribbon. While
the ribbon is pinned, you can collapse it by clicking the
up arrow that replaces the pushpin at the far right of the
ribbon, and expand it again by clicking the down arrow
that appears in the same position. To unpin the ribbon,
collapse it and then click any tab.

Displaying Item Check Boxes
The other check box option in the Show/hide group is
Item check boxes. When enabled, this option displays
a check box on or near an item when you point to the
item in the file list pane, and also when the item is
selected. You can use these check boxes to select or
deselect multiple files. File selection is covered in Skill 5
of this chapter.

Skill 3
Create and Rename a File or Folder

You create data files when you save your work in an application. For example, when you save your work in Word, you create a document file. Windows also allows you to create certain types of empty data files without opening an application. You will use that technique to create data files for this skill.

Most people store their data files in one of the user folders that Windows provides, such as Documents or Pictures. To organize your work, you might also create folders within those user folders. For example, within

the Pictures folder, you might create a folder called Vacations. You can also create folders in locations other than the user folders. For example, you might create a Projects folder on a flash drive.

It's generally safe to rename files and folders that you created, as well as most data files. However, avoid renaming files or folders associated with applications, such as those in the Program Files folder. If you rename a file that runs an application, or a helper file for that application, the application might not work correctly.

---

1. Open File Explorer if it is not already open.

2-3 Another Way
Right-click the Start button, point to *Shut down or sign out*, and then click *Sign out*.

TIP
Expand *This PC* in the Navigation pane and then click *Documents*.

2. Click *This PC* in the Navigation pane.

3. Double-click the *Documents* folder in the file list pane.

Documents

Step 3

4. Click the Home tab and then click the New folder button in the New group to display a new folder in the file list pane, with the default name *New folder* highlighted.

5. Type Financial to replace the highlighted folder name.

Financial

Step 5

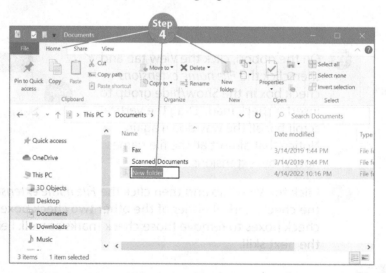

6 Another Way
Click in a blank area in the file list pane, away from the new folder.

6. Press Enter to accept the new folder name.

7. Click the *Financial* folder to select it, if it is not already selected.

Financial

Step 7

8 Another Way
Right-click the *Financial* folder and then click *Rename*.

8. On the ribbon, click the Home tab and then click the Rename button in the Organize group.

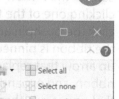

⑨ Type W10-Reference and then press Enter.

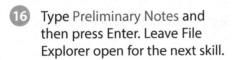
Step 9

⑩ Double-click the *W10-Reference* folder to open it.

11-13 *Another Way*
Right-click the Start button, point to *Shut down or sign out*, and then click *Sign out*.

⑪ Right-click anywhere in the file list pane.

⑫ Point to *New* on the shortcut menu to open a secondary shortcut submenu.

⑬ Click *Text Document* on the submenu. A new text document appears in the file list pane.

TIP
If you are creating a file or folder that will be part of a website, avoid including a space in the name because spaces can cause problems in web addresses.

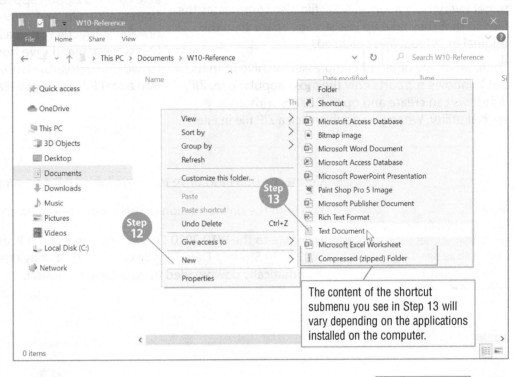

The content of the shortcut submenu you see in Step 13 will vary depending on the applications installed on the computer.

⑭ Type Notes and then press Enter.

15 *Another Way*
With the Notes file still selected, press the F2 key.

⑮ Right-click the *Notes* file and then click *Rename*.

⑯ Type Preliminary Notes and then press Enter. Leave File Explorer open for the next skill.

Skill Extra

Guidelines for Renaming Files and Folders

You can rename files and folders as needed. Windows allows file and folder names of up to 255 characters, including letters, numbers, symbols, and spaces. (Some applications have a limit of 255 characters for the whole path, not just the file name, so keep names short whenever possible.) A few symbols can't be a part of a file or folder name: the forward and backward slashes (/ and \), pipe symbol (|), question mark and asterisk (? and *), opening and closing angle brackets (< and >), quotation mark ("), and colon (:). A file name may contain periods, however, as in This.is.my.file.docx. (Note that the final period in this file name is part of the extension, *.docx*, rather than the file name.)

Skill 4
Download and Extract Student Data Files

To complete the exercises and assignments in this textbook, you must download the student data files from the online course. All the files you will need are bundled into a single ZIP file. A *ZIP file* is a compressed archive file with a *.zip* extension. A ZIP file stores multiple files in a single container file that you can work with as a whole, so you only have to download one file to get everything at once. A ZIP file also compresses the files so that they take up less storage space than the original individual files occupied.

There are many different compressed archive formats, but Windows supports only the most popular one, ZIP. Windows can create and open ZIP files without any special utility. When you double-click a ZIP file in File Explorer, its content is displayed in the same way as the contents of a folder.

Although a ZIP file behaves much like a folder in Windows, it is not actually a folder, and you may run into a few limitations when working with zipped content in File Explorer. For example, you might not be able to run a zipped application without extracting it from the ZIP file, and some types of data files may not preview correctly within a ZIP file. Although most data files will open and save from within a ZIP file, it is better to avoid any possible issues by extracting the data files into a real folder, as you learn to do in this skill.

1️⃣ Connect a USB flash drive to an available USB port on your computer.

TIP

Google Chrome is the preferred web browser for Cirrus. If you have trouble accessing Cirrus with a different browser, switching to Chrome may resolve the problem.

2️⃣ Log in to the online version of this course using a web browser.

3️⃣ Navigate to the W10 2020 Course Resources module and click the W10 2020 Student Data Files link in the list of activities. A zipped archive file is automatically downloaded to your local computer.

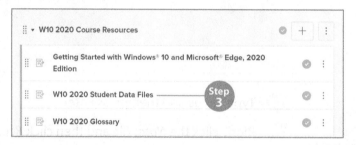

4️⃣ Click the file that appears at the bottom of the browser window.

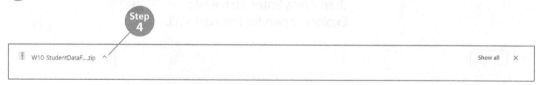

TIP

Because W10-StudentDataFiles is a ZIP file, it opens using File Explorer. If you were downloading some other type of file, it would open in an application appropriate for that file.

5️⃣ In File Explorer, click the Extract Compressed Folder Tools tab if necessary to make it active and then click the Extract all button.

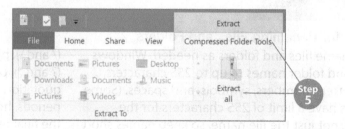

---

6 In the Extract Compressed (Zipped) Folders dialog box, click the Browse button and then navigate to your USB flash drive.

7 Click the Select Folder button to return to the Extract Compressed (Zipped) Folders dialog box.

TIP
You will learn about uploading files to OneDrive in Chapter 4, Skills 1 and 4.

8 Click the Extract button in the dialog box. The files are extracted and copied to your USB flash drive in a folder named W10-StudentDataFiles.

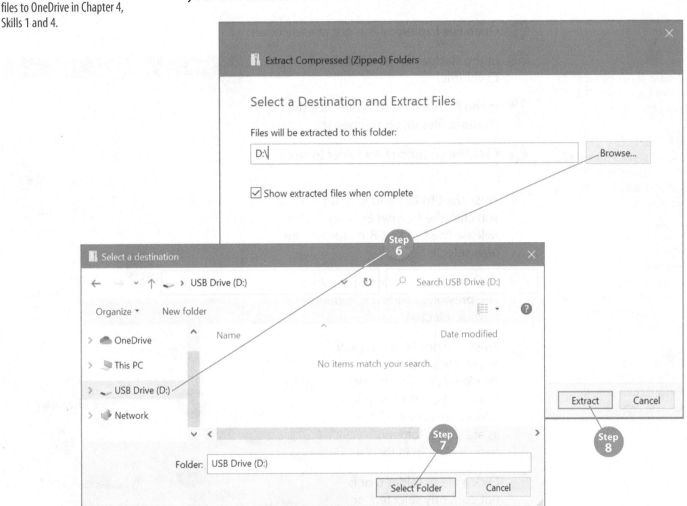

9 Close all but one File Explorer window and the browser window. Leave the remaining File Explorer window open for the next skill.

10 Disconnect your USB flash drive.

Skill Extra

Downloading Executable Files

Not every file you download will be a ZIP file. Some files you download will be *executable files* (with an *.exe* extension) that run programs when you double-click them. For example, you might download a setup program that installs or updates an application on your computer. Beware of downloading executable files from untrusted websites or unknown sources such as emails. They may contain viruses or other harmful software.

Skill 5
Select Multiple Files and Folders

Many actions, such as copying and deleting, can be performed on more than one file or folder at once. Before performing the action, you must make a multiple-item selection. All the items you select to be acted on as a group must be in the same location. For example, you can select a folder and three files that are all in the same folder, but you cannot select two files in different folders.

TIP

If you do not see the C: volume in Step 2, double-click *This PC* to expand the list.

TIP

Some of the folders are specific to the hardware in the PC. You might see different folders than the ones shown here.

TIP

Pressing and holding Ctrl while clicking enables you to select multiple noncontiguous files or folders—that is, two or more files or folders that are not next to each other in a list.

TIP

You may need to scroll down in the file list pane to see the folders in Steps 5–7.

1. Open File Explorer if it is not already open.

2. In the Navigation pane, click the C: volume.

3. In the file list pane, double-click the *Program Files* folder to open it.

4. Click the *Common Files* folder to select it.

5. Press the Ctrl key and hold it down as you click the *Internet Explorer* folder. Release the Ctrl key. Both folders are now selected.

6. Click the *Windows Defender* folder. The previously selected folders are now deselected.

7. Press and hold the Shift key as you click the *WindowsPowerShell* folder. Release the Shift key. Both folders are now selected, as are all the folders between them in the list.

8. Click a file or folder that is not currently selected, or an empty area of the file list pane, to deselect the selected folders. Leave File Explorer open for the next skill.

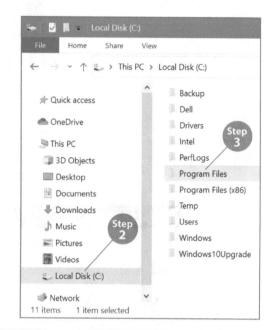

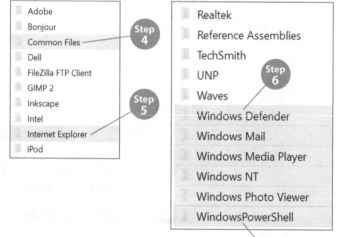

Skill Extra

Selecting Multiple Items with the Keyboard

You can also select multiple files and folders with the keyboard. To select noncontiguous items using the arrow keys: Highlight the first item you wish to select. Press and hold the Ctrl key while using the arrow keys to move to the next item, and then tap the Spacebar to select the item. Continue pressing and holding the Ctrl key, and using the arrow keys and Spacebar, until you have selected all the desired items. To select a contiguous block of items using the keyboard: Highlight the first item, and then press the Shift key and hold it down while using the arrow keys to extend the selection.

Create a Compressed Archive (ZIP) File

Windows makes it easy for you to create your own ZIP files. You might create a compressed archive file containing all your completed assignments for the week, for example, and then send that file to your instructor for grading. ZIP files simplify the process of transferring multiple files because they make it possible for you to work with the group as you would a single file.

TIP

Complete Skill 4 of this chapter if you have not yet downloaded the student data files to your USB flash drive.

1. Connect your USB flash drive containing the student data files.

2. Click the File Explorer button on the Windows taskbar to open File Explorer if it is not already open.

3. Double-click *This PC* in the Navigation pane if necessary to expand the list.

4. Click your USB flash drive in the Navigation pane.

5. In the file list pane, double-click the *W10-StudentDataFiles* folder to open it.

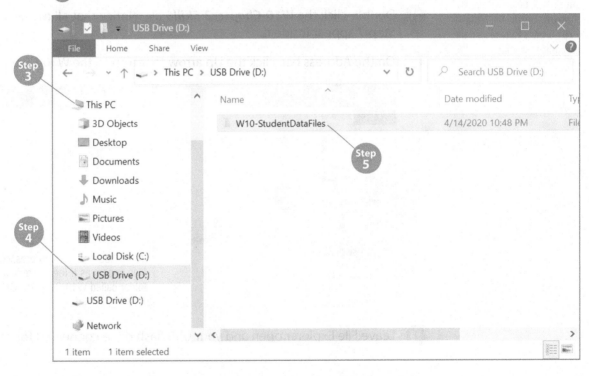

6. In the file list pane, double-click the *W10-Chapter2* folder to open it.

TIP

See Skill 5 of this chapter for steps on selecting multiple files.

7. Select the four files in the *W10-Chapter2* folder.

TIP

The icons next to the image files in Step 7 may vary depending on the applications installed on your PC.

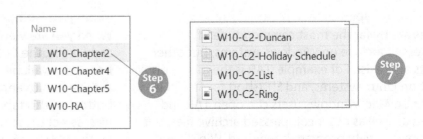

8-9 **Another Way**
Right-click the selected files,
point to *Send to*, and then click
Compressed (zipped) folder.

8 Click the Share tab on the ribbon.

9 Click the Zip button in the Send group.

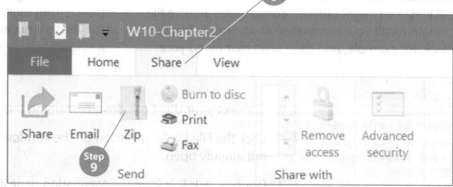

TIP

If you accidentally pressed Enter
after Step 9, before you get a
chance to rename the file in
Step 10, press F2 to reopen the
file name for editing.

10 Type W10-Chapter2-Skill6 and then press Enter to rename the new ZIP file.

11 Double-click the **W10-Chapter2-Skill6** file. Notice that all the files you selected in Step 7 appear inside it.

12 On the Address bar, click the Up arrow to return to the W10-Chapter2 folder.

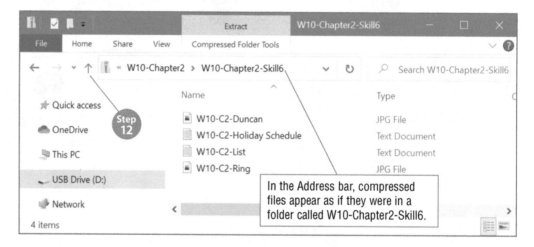

In the Address bar, compressed files appear as if they were in a folder called W10-Chapter2-Skill6.

13 Leave File Explorer open and your USB flash drive connected for the next skill.

Skill Extras

Using Other Types of Compressed Archives
ZIP files are by far the most common type of
compressed archive on Windows systems, but other
formats also exist. For example, TAR is the most popular
format on Linux systems, and SIT (short for *StuffIt*) is
popular on Mac. Windows users can open TAR and
SIT files, as well as other compressed archive files, but
a third-party utility program is required. WinZIP and
7-Zip are popular programs you can use to open many
different types of compressed archives.

Managing Compressed Archive Files
When you are viewing the contents of a compressed
archive file, the Compressed Folder Tools Extract tab
becomes available on the ribbon. To extract all the
archive files to another location, click the Extract all
button on this tab. To extract one or more individual
files, select those files within the archive and then
on the ribbon's Extract tab, click one of the location
shortcuts (such as *Documents* or *Desktop*) that appear in
the Extract To group.

Skill 7
Move and Copy Files

You may sometimes need to move or copy data files between locations. For example, you might transfer a file from the Documents folder on your home computer to a USB flash drive to take it to school. Copying, as the name implies, leaves the file in its original location and places a copy of it in the destination location. Moving removes the file from the original location.

The two most common ways to move and copy files in Windows are to drag-and-drop and to use the Windows Clipboard. When you *drag-and-drop* files, both the original location and the destination must be visible in File Explorer. The destination can be visible as a separate File Explorer window or as a shortcut in the Navigation pane. If the original location and the destination are on the same volume, the default is a move operation. If they are not on the same volume, the default is a copy operation. You can force a move operation regardless of the default by pressing Shift as you drag, or force a copy operation by pressing Ctrl as you drag.

The *Clipboard* is a temporary holding area in memory. When you select a file and then issue the Cut or Copy command, the selection is either moved or copied to the Clipboard. You then display the destination location and issue the Paste command to complete the operation.

Your hard disk contains both data files and program files. A *data file* is a file you create in an application to store your work; a *program file* is a file that runs a program. You should move only data files, not program files. If you move a program file, or any of its helper files, the program might not run correctly.

Move and Copy Using Drag-and-Drop

1 Make sure your USB flash drive containing the student data files is connected and File Explorer is open.

2 In the Navigation pane, click the USB flash drive to display its contents.

3 Right-click the USB flash drive to display a shortcut menu.

4 Click *Open in new window* on the shortcut menu. A new File Explorer window opens, showing the same location.

TIP

See Chapter 1, Skill 4, if you need help sizing and arranging windows.

5 Size and arrange the windows so they are side by side and the file list panes of both windows are visible. Position the newly opened window to the left.

6 In the file list pane of the left window, double-click the *W10-StudentDataFiles* folder.

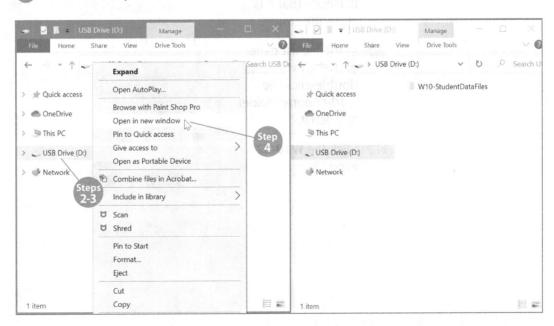

7 In the Navigation pane of the right window, double-click *Quick access* to expand it if needed, and then click the *Documents* folder.

8 Drag-and-drop the W10-Chapter2 folder from the file list pane in the left window to the file list pane in the right window. Because the locations are on different volumes, dragging-and-dropping copies the folder.

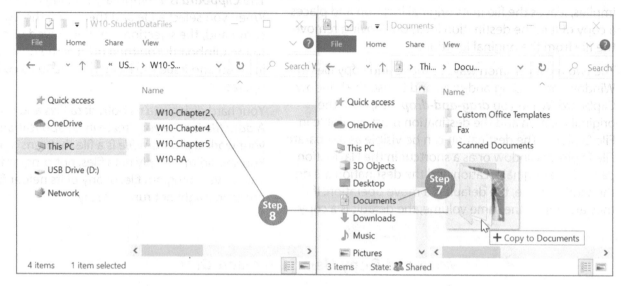

Move and Copy Using Copy and Paste

9 In the Navigation pane of the right window, click the USB flash drive to redisplay its contents.

10 Click the Home tab and then click the New folder button to create a new folder.

11 Type W10-Backup.

12 Press Enter.

13 Double-click the new folder to open it. Notice that it is currently empty.

14 In the file list pane of the left window, double-click the *W10-Chapter2* folder to open it.

15 Click the **W10-C2-Ring** file.

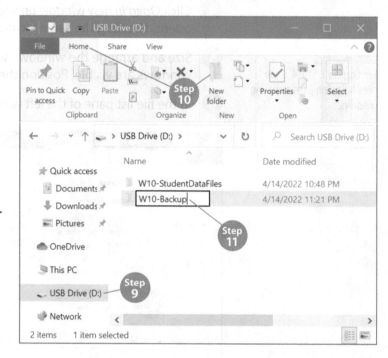

16 *Another Way*
Click the file and then press Ctrl + C.
OR
Right-click the file and then click *Copy* on the shortcut menu.

17 *Another Way*
Click a blank area in the file list pane of the W10-Backup window and then press Ctrl + V.
OR
Right-click a blank area in the file list pane of the W10-Backup window and then click *Paste* on the shortcut menu.

TIP
To move a file with the Clipboard rather than copying it, click the Cut button in the Clipboard group.

16 Click the Home tab and then click the Copy button in the Clipboard group.

17 Click the right window to make it active, click the Home tab, and then click the Paste button in the Clipboard group. The copied file is pasted from the Clipboard into the W10-Backup folder.

18 Close the left window (the W10-Chapter2 window).

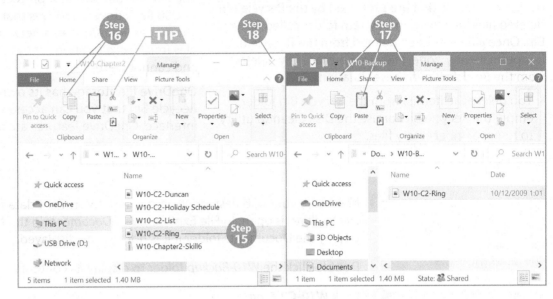

19 In the Navigation pane of the remaining File Explorer window, click the USB flash drive to return to its top level.

20 Click the *W10-Backup* folder, if it is not already selected.

21 On the Home tab, click the Copy button.

22 In the Navigation pane, click *Documents*.

23 On the Home tab, click the Paste button. Leave your USB flash drive connected and File Explorer open for the next skill.

Skill Extras

Using the Move To and Copy To Buttons
On the Home tab of the ribbon, you'll find buttons that provide an alternative way to move and copy. To move a file, click the file to select it, click the Home tab, click the Move to button in the Organize group, and then click the desired location on the shortcut menu. If you don't see the location you want on the shortcut menu, click *Choose location*, browse to the desired location in the dialog box, and then click the Move button.

Working with Navigation Pane Locations
If the desired destination location appears as an icon on the Navigation pane, you can drag-and-drop a file or folder onto that icon to move or copy it to that destination. The shortcuts in the Quick access list on the Navigation pane are especially useful, because they include folders you have used recently or frequently.

Skill 8
Delete Files and Use the Recycle Bin

To save storage space and keep your files organized, you might delete some files. For example, when you are finished with this textbook, you might delete the student data files that you downloaded. Even after a file or folder has been deleted, you might be able to get it back. On volumes that are protected by the Recycle Bin, deleted files are stored in a system folder called Recycle Bin. Once a file has been deleted from the Recycle Bin, it is permanently gone. Files are permanently deleted from the Recycle Bin in these situations:

- You delete the item(s) from the Recycle Bin folder, empty the Recycle Bin, or use the Disk Cleanup utility to remove unnecessary files.

- The Recycle Bin exceeds its preset size limit, or the hard disk on which it is stored becomes nearly full. In either case, Windows automatically deletes files from the Recycle Bin, beginning with the oldest files.

The Recycle Bin does not protect external drives, such as USB flash drives, or drives that you access via the internet or your local area network. When you delete files from those locations, they are permanently deleted and cannot be retrieved.

OneDrive file storage has its own separate online Recycle Bin that you can access via OneDrive's web interface. OneDrive features are discussed in Chapter 4.

TIP

The Documents folder contains at least three folders that you placed there in earlier skills: W10-Backup, W10-Chapter2, and W10-Reference. It may also contain other folders.

3-4 *Another Way*
Right-click the file and then click *Delete*.
OR
Click the file and then press the Delete key.

TIP

If you are prompted for confirmation when you click the Delete button in Step 4, click Yes.

TIP

To bypass the Recycle Bin when deleting an item and delete it permanently, you can press Shift + Delete rather than just Delete.

1. Make sure your USB flash drive containing the student data files is connected and File Explorer is open. In File Explorer, click *Documents* in the Navigation pane to display the Documents folder if it is not already displayed.

2. Double-click the *W10-Backup* folder to display its contents.

3. Click **W10-C2-Ring**.

4. Click the Home tab and then click the Delete button in the Organize group. This moves the file to the Recycle Bin.

5. Double-click the Recycle Bin icon on the desktop to open the Recycle Bin window.

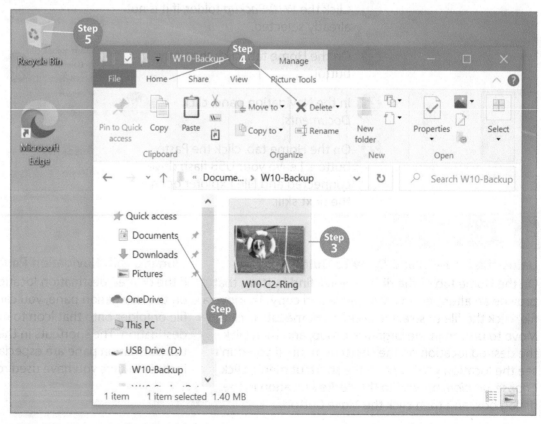

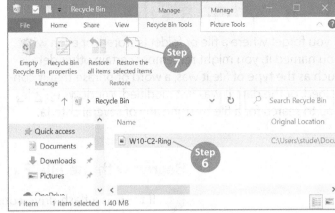

TIP

Your Recycle Bin might contain other files besides W10-C2-Ring. You may need to scroll to locate the file.

TIP

If Windows has no default application for the type of file being restored, you might see a message asking what application to use to open the file. Select a default application and click OK. If the file opens in the chosen application, close the application. Then repeat Step 7.

11 *Another Way*
Right-click the Recycle Bin icon on the desktop, and then click *Empty Recycle Bin*.

TIP

Before you click Yes in Step 12, confirm there is nothing in the Recycle Bin that you want to retrieve.

TIP

When you try to delete a file from your USB flash drive in Step 16, a confirmation box appears because the Recycle Bin does not protect external drives.

6 In the Recycle Bin window, click *W10-C2-Ring* to select it.

7 On the Manage Recycle Bin Tools tab, click the Restore the selected items button in the Restore group. The file returns to its original location in the W10-Backup folder.

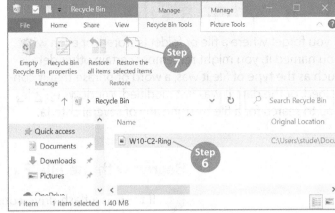

8 Click the W10-Backup window to make it active, and then click *Documents* in the Navigation pane to return to that folder.

9 In the file list pane, click the *W10-Backup* folder if it is not already selected, press and hold down the Ctrl key, click the *W10-Reference* folder, and then release the Ctrl key. Both folders are selected.

10 On the Home tab, click the Delete button to move those folders to the Recycle Bin.

11 Click the Recycle Bin window to make it active, and then, on the Manage Recycle Bin Tools tab, click the Empty Recycle Bin button in the Manage group.

12 In the Delete Multiple Items dialog box, click Yes to confirm. Everything in the Recycle Bin is permanently deleted.

13 Close the Recycle Bin window.

14 In the Navigation pane of the remaining File Explorer window, click your USB flash drive to display its contents.

15 In the file list pane, click the *W10-Backup* folder and then press the Delete key.

16 Click Yes to confirm the deletion.

17 Make sure all file operations have completed, and then disconnect your USB flash drive from the PC. Leave File Explorer open for the next skill if it doesn't close automatically.

Skill Extra

Turning Off Deletion Confirmations

If you see a confirmation box asking if you want to move the item or items to the Recycle Bin, it means that deletion confirmation is enabled. To turn off deletion confirmation, on the ribbon, click the Home tab, click the Delete button arrow, and then click *Show recycle confirmation* in the drop-down list.

Skill 9

Search for a File

If you forget where a file or folder is stored, or even what you named it, you might remember certain other details such as the type of file it was, a word or phrase that it contained, or the date it was last modified. Windows enables you to search for a file by using any of several criteria.

There are two ways to search for a file in Windows: by using the search box in File Explorer or by using the search box on the taskbar.

Search with the File Explorer Search Box

1 If there is a flash drive connected to the PC, disconnect it. Open File Explorer if it is not already open.

TIP

Navigating to a certain location, as you do in Step 2, confines the search to that location and its subfolders. This can make the search run faster.

2 In the Navigation pane, click *Documents*.

3 Click in the File Explorer search box, type List, and then press Enter. The search begins immediately, listing all the files in the Documents folder that contain the word *List* in their names. Wait for the search to complete.

4 In the search results, click **W10-C2-List**.

5 On the ribbon, click the Search Tools Search tab and then click the Open file location button in the Options group. File Explorer switches to show the contents of the W10-Chapter2 folder and the Search tab disappears.

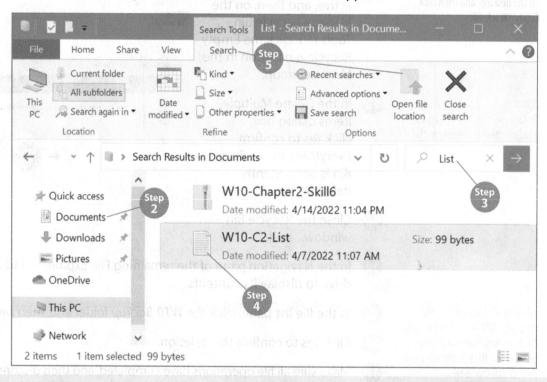

Searching Inside Files

To speed up searches and eliminate many false positives, Windows does not look inside a file when performing a search with File Explorer. For example, if a text file named Vacation.txt contains the word *holiday*, a search for the word *holiday* will not find that file. However, you can configure Search to look inside files as needed. On the Search Tools Search tab in the Options group, click the Advanced options button arrow and then click *File contents* in the drop-down list to toggle on that option. Repeat the same sequence of steps to toggle the option off again when you are finished with your search.

6 In the File Explorer search box, type Windows and then press Enter. No search results are found because you are currently searching only within the W10-Chapter2 folder.

7 Click the Search Tools Search tab and then click the This PC button in the Location group. The search reruns, searching the entire PC rather than just the W10-Chapter2 folder. This time, many results are found.

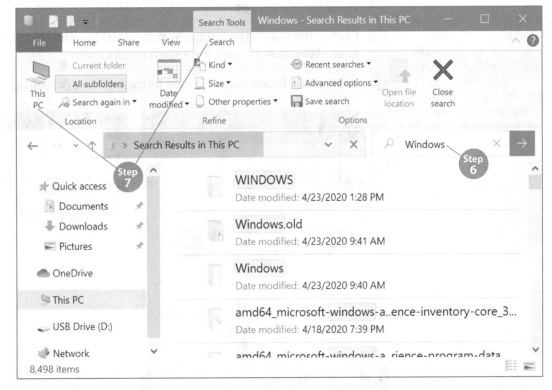

8 Click the Search Tools Search tab, and then click the Kind button arrow in the Refine group.

9 Click *Folder* in the drop-down list. The search results are filtered to show only folders with *Windows* in their names.

10 Close File Explorer.

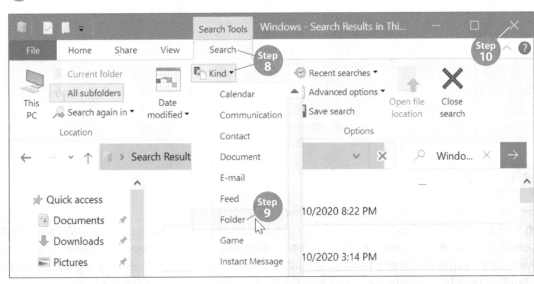

Search with the Search Box

TIP

You do not have to wait for Windows to finish searching before going on to Step 12.

11 Click in the search box on the Windows taskbar and then type W10-C2-Duncan. Windows displays the search results.

12 At the top of the results list, click *W10-C2-Duncan JPG File*. The picture opens in the Photos app.

TIP

In Step 12, the file opens in your default photo-handling app, which is probably Photos. If your system has a different default set, it might open in a different app. If you are prompted to specify how you want to open the file, choose the Photos app.

13 Close the Photos app.

14 Click in the search box on the Windows taskbar and then type W10-C2-Duncan again. Windows displays the search results again.

15 Point to the found picture to see its location in a ScreenTip.

TIP

In Step 15, the location you see in the ScreenTip may be different.

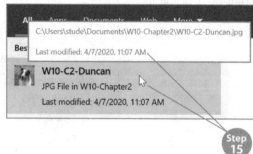

16 Click away from the search results pane to close it.

Skill Extra

Searching the Web with the Search Box

In Skill 9, you learned to use Windows' search box to search your own files. You can also use it to search the web for information on any topic you want to know about. Type a term or phrase describing the topic in the search box on the Windows taskbar, and then click *Web* at the top of the search results pane to search online. You will learn more about searching using the Search box in Chapter 3.

Tasks Summary

Task	Button/Option	Action
close File Explorer	[X]	In upper right corner of File Explorer, click Close (X) button.
copy and paste files using Clipboard	Copy Paste	In File Explorer window, select files, click Copy button in Clipboard group on Home tab, go to destination folder, click Paste button.
copy files using drag-and-drop	Copy to Documents / Documents	In File Explorer, open windows for source and destination volume folders, select files in source folder, press and hold Ctrl key while dragging files to destination folder.
create and name ZIP file	Zip	In file list pane of File Explorer window, select files. On Share tab, click Zip button in Send group, type name, press Enter.
create and name new file		In file list pane of File Explorer window, right-click a blank area, point to *New*, click document type, type name, press Enter.
create and name new folder		On Quick Access Toolbar in File Explorer window, click New folder button, type name, press Enter.
delete file	Delete	In file list pane of File Explorer window, click Home tab, click Delete button in Organize group.
empty Recycle Bin	Empty Recycle Bin	On desktop, double-click Recycle Bin icon. In Recycle Bin window, click Manage Recycle Bin Tools tab, click Empty Recycle Bin button in Manage group, close Recycle Bin window.
expand or collapse Navigation pane item	> ∨	In Navigation pane of File Explorer window, click right arrow next to item to expand listing or down arrow to collapse it.
go backward, forward, and up one level in folder structure	← → ∨ ↑	In Address bar of File Explorer window, click Back arrow to go to previous location, click Forward arrow to go to next location, click Up arrow to go up one level.
move files using drag-and-drop		Open separate File Explorer windows for source folder in one volume and destination folder in another volume, select files in source folder, press and hold Shift key while dragging files to destination folder.
open File Explorer		On Windows taskbar, click File Explorer button.
rename file or folder	Rename	In File Explorer window, click file or folder, click Rename button in Organize group on Home tab (or press F2), type new name, press Enter.
restore file from Recycle Bin	Restore the selected items	On desktop, double-click Recycle Bin icon. In Recycle Bin window, click file, click Recycle Bin Tools Manage tab, click Restore the selected items button in Restore group, close Recycle Bin window.
search for file using File Explorer	Search Documents 🔍	In Navigation pane of File Explorer window, click storage location to search, click in File Explorer search box, type file name.
select multiple contiguous files		In file list pane of File Explorer window, click first file, press and hold Shift key, click last file, release Shift key.
select multiple noncontiguous files		In file list pane of File Explorer window, click first file, press and hold Ctrl key, click additional files, release Ctrl key.
show/hide file name extensions and/or hidden items	☐ File name extensions ☐ Hidden items	On ribbon in File Explorer window, click View tab, click *File name extensions* and/or *Hidden items* check boxes in Show/hide group.
unpack ZIP file	Extract all	In File Explorer window, select file, click Compressed Folder Tools Extract tab, click Extract all button, select folder, click Extract button.

Chapter **3**

Getting Information from the Internet

The heart of the internet is a system of interconnected file servers called the *web* (short for *worldwide web*). Web servers store individual data files called *web pages*, each of which has a unique address, called a *uniform resource locator (URL)*. If you know a web page's URL, you can view that page using *web browser* software on almost any computing device that has internet access. A collection of related pages is known as a *website*.

Windows 10 comes with the *Microsoft Edge* browser. Edge is an alternative to Internet Explorer (IE), which is Microsoft's full-featured browser that has been included with Microsoft Windows for over two decades. You can access the web with a different browser, such as Google Chrome or Mozilla Firefox, if you like. However, because Microsoft Edge is the default browser in Windows 10, it is the browser you will learn about in this chapter.

TIP

With the May 2020 update to Windows 10, Microsoft released a new and improved version of Edge. On systems that have not been updated to the latest version of Windows 10, Edge may work slightly differently than described in this chapter.

Skills You Learn

1 Get Started with the Microsoft Edge Browser

2 Use Tabbed Browsing

3 Use Search Engines to Find Content

4 Download a File from a Website

5 Save and Reopen Favorites

6 Review Browser History and Clear Browsing Data

7 Print a Web Page

8 Use Windows Search to Get Information Online

Files You Use

For these skills, you do not need any student data files.

Skill 1
Get Started with the Microsoft Edge Browser

The Microsoft Edge browser is the default browser in Windows 10, so when you click a link to a web page in a document or email message, the web page opens in Microsoft Edge. You can also launch Microsoft Edge from its button on the Windows taskbar or from its shortcut on the Start menu or on the desktop.

The Microsoft Edge interface is very spare and clean. Just a few buttons appear on a simple toolbar, and a search

box and an Address bar allow you to type URLs for the pages you want to visit and locate information on any topic.

Even though Microsoft Edge is the primary browser in Windows 10, Internet Explorer remains available to use to view older web pages that might not load correctly in Edge.

---

1 *Another Way*
On the Windows taskbar, click in the search box, type Microsoft Edge, and then click *Microsoft Edge Microsoft recommended browser* in the search results list.

TIP
If you see a floating Live Help box when you open the page in Step 3, you can close it by clicking its Close (X) button.

1 On the Windows taskbar, click the Microsoft Edge button to start the Microsoft Edge browser.

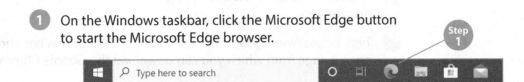

2 Click in the Address bar and then type https://ParadigmEducation.com.

3 Press Enter to open the Paradigm Education Solutions home page.

4 In the navigation bar on the web page, click *ABOUT* to view the About Paradigm page on the same website.

5 Click the Back arrow to return to the previously viewed page—in this case, the Paradigm Education Solutions home page.

TIP
You can click the Refresh button to reload a web page that hasn't loaded correctly or to download an updated version of the page if it has changed since you last loaded it.

6 Click the Forward arrow to go forward to view the About Paradigm page again.

7 Click the Refresh button to reload the page. Leave Microsoft Edge open for the next skill.

Skill Extra

Navigating in Other Browsers
Windows 10 allows you to download and run other web browsers. The most popular alternatives for Windows users are Google Chrome and Mozilla Firefox. Microsoft's earlier browser, Internet Explorer, is also available in Windows 10. Each of these browsers has the same navigation features as Microsoft Edge, including Back, Forward, and Refresh buttons.

Skill 2
Use Tabbed Browsing

With Microsoft Edge, and most other modern browsers, you can have more than one web page open at once, each on its own tab in the browser window. You can click a tab to switch to that page, or close a tab when you are finished working with it.

1 With Microsoft Edge open, click in the Address bar, type https://www.microsoft.com/en-us, and then press Enter.

2 Click the New tab button to open a new browser tab.

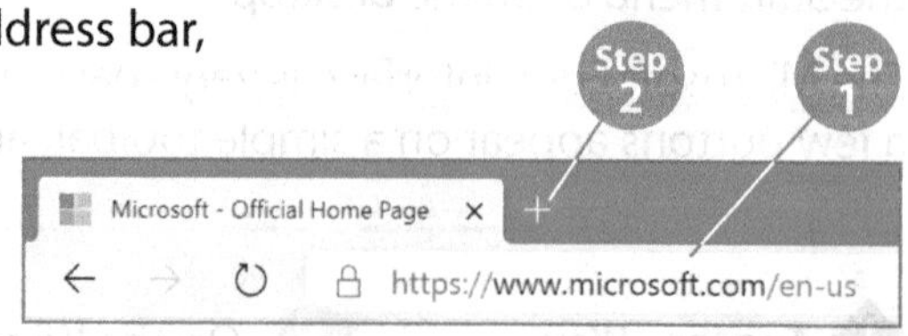

3 Type https://www.google.com/chrome/ in the Address bar and then press Enter to open a page from which you can download the Google Chrome browser.

4 Click the New tab button to open another new tab.

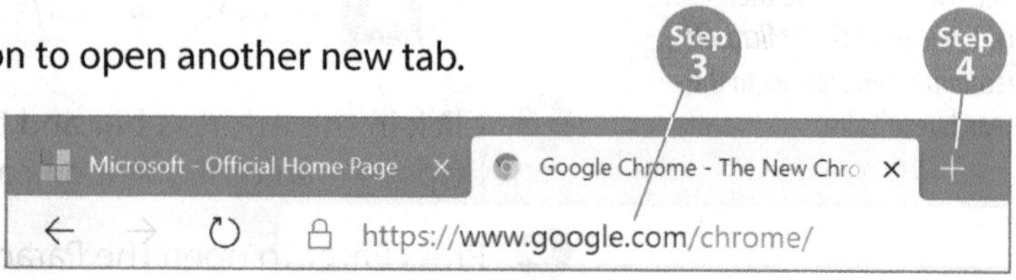

5 Type https://www.firefox.com in the Address bar and then press Enter to open the Firefox Browser home page.

TIP

Don't worry that what you typed in Step 5 changes when the page loads. Many sites redirect your request to other pages, as explained in the Skill Extra below.

6 *Another Way*
Press Ctrl + W.

6 Click the Close tab button to close the Download Firefox tab.

> The URL you type in Step 5 redirects to this address.

7 Right-click the Google Chrome tab and then click *Duplicate tab* on the shortcut menu. Now there are two identical Google Chrome tabs.

8 Right-click the new Google Chrome tab and then click *Close other tabs* on the shortcut menu to close all the other tabs. Leave Microsoft Edge open for the next skill.

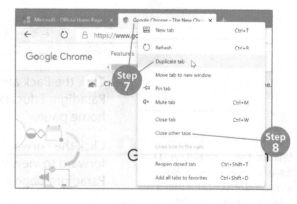

Skill Extra

Understanding Redirects

When you type a URL, the website may redirect you to a different address. Websites use redirects for many different reasons. For example, when you type the address *https://www.firefox.com*, you are redirected to the URL shown in the image for Step 6 above, which is the website for Mozilla, the parent company of the Firefox browser. Some websites redirect to different versions depending on the browser you are using; for example, you may be redirected to a version optimized for viewing on a mobile device.

Skill 3
Use Search Engines to Find Content

Sometimes you might have a URL to manually type into the Address bar to open a particular site, but more often you will not know the exact URL for the content you want to see. You can use a search engine to search the internet for what you want. A *search engine* is a website or service that is dedicated to maintaining a searchable directory of web content. To use a search engine, you can navigate to its website and type keywords in the search box. Most browsers are allied with a particular search engine. For example, when you type in the Microsoft Edge search box, the browser uses the Microsoft search engine, Bing. However, you can use any search engine with any browser. To use another search engine, navigate to its website and then type keywords in the search box at that site.

1 With Microsoft Edge open, click in the Address bar, type mla research paper, and then press Enter to display the search results.

TIP

If Microsoft Edge tries to auto-complete the address with extra text in Step 2, press the space bar once after typing https:// www.google.com but before pressing Enter.

2 Click in the Address bar, type https://www.google.com, and then press Enter to open the Google search engine home page.

TIP

The graphic you see on the Google search page may vary; it changes on certain days to celebrate holidays and birthdays of famous people.

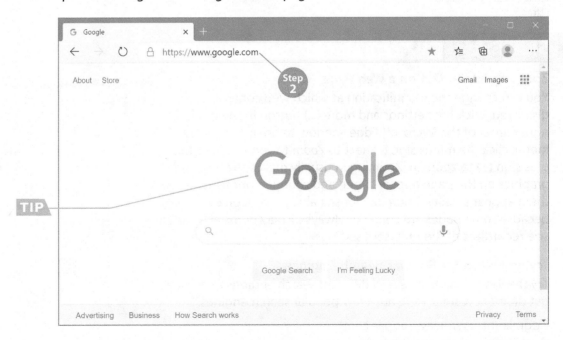

3 Type mla research paper in the search box and then press Enter.

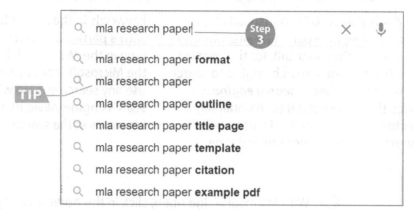

4 In the search results, click any item that interests you to display that page. Leave Microsoft Edge open for the next skill.

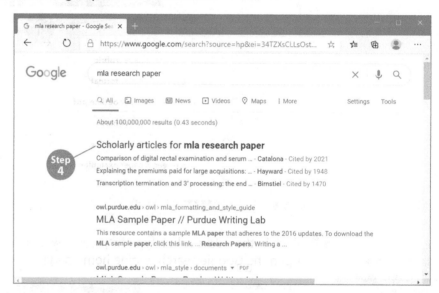

Skill Extras

Zooming In and Out on a Web Page

You can change the magnification at which web content is displayed. Click the Settings and more (...) button in the upper right corner of the Microsoft Edge window to open a menu. On the menu, click the minus sign (–) next to *Zoom* to zoom out, or the plus sign (+) to zoom in. Zooming in usually makes the text and graphics on the page appear larger, and zooming out usually makes them appear smaller. Zooming doesn't always work on every page because some pages are coded to always display items at a certain size regardless of the browser's settings.

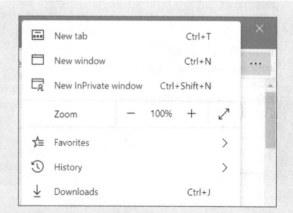

Trying Out Other Popular Search Engines

Try the same search in several different search engines to see if you get different results. Here are a few popular search engines.

Dogpile (https://www.dogpile.com)
DuckDuckGo (https://duckduckgo.com)
Yahoo! (https://www.yahoo.com)

Skill 4
Download a File from a Website

Not all hyperlinks open web pages. Some of them initiate file downloads when you click them. When you download a file with Microsoft Edge, the downloaded file is placed in your personal Downloads folder (C: > Users > *username* > Downloads, where *username* is your account). After the download has completed, you can use the Downloads list in Microsoft Edge to access your downloaded file.

①　With Microsoft Edge open, click in the Address bar, type https://W10 .Paradigm Education.com/Riley, and then press Enter to open the Agility Trial Champion web page.

②　In the *To download Riley's pedigree information* line, click the <u>click here</u> hyperlink. The download begins automatically.

③　Wait for the file to finish downloading. You can see its progress in the status bar at the bottom of the Edge window. When it is finished, an <u>Open file</u> hyperlink appears under its name.

④　Click the Show all button to display the Downloads list.

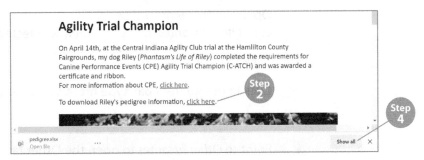

⑤　Click the Close tab (X) button on the Downloads tab to close the Downloads list.

⑥　Click the Settings and more (...) button to open its menu.

⑦ **Another Way**
You can also press Ctrl + J to open the Downloads list.

⑦　Click *Downloads* to open the Downloads list.

⑧　Click the Close tab (X) icon on the Downloads tab to close it again. Leave Microsoft Edge open to the Agility Trial Champion web page for the next skill.

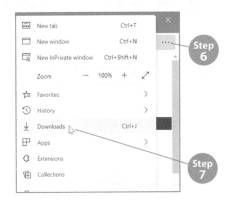

Skill Extra

Reducing the Risk of Malware in Downloads

Be cautious when downloading files from websites. Most downloaded data files (pictures, documents, and so on) are fine. However, a downloaded executable file (that is, a file that runs a program) might contain *malware* that could harm your system or install nuisance software that displays ads. Generally, you should download executable files only from websites that you know and trust.

Skill 5
Save and Reopen Favorites

You can save the URLs of pages you want to visit again later, and then choose them from a list in your browser. The names used for the list and its items vary depending on your browser. Microsoft Edge calls it the *Favorites list* and calls each item a *favorite*. Most other browsers call it the *Bookmark list* and call individual items on the list *bookmarks*.

The URLs you add to your Favorites list are associated with your Windows user account. This means that anyone else signing into the same computer using a different account will not see your favorites but will instead see their own.

TIP

If the Agility Trial Champion web page is not open when you start this skill, repeat Skill 4, Step 1 to open it.

1. With Microsoft Edge open to the Agility Trial Champion web page, click the Add this page to favorites button to open the Favorite added dialog box.

2. Type Riley's Award to replace the text that appears in the *Name* box.

3. Open the *Folder* drop-down list and click *Other favorites*, if it is not already selected.

4. Click the Done button.

5. Click in the Address bar, type https://ParadigmEducation.com, and then press Enter.

6. Click the Favorites button.

TIP

The Other favorites list might open to the left of the Favorites menu rather than to the right as shown in Step 7.

7. Point to *Other favorites* to open the Other favorites list.

8. Click *Riley's Award* in the Other favorites list to reopen that page. Leave Microsoft Edge open for the next skill.

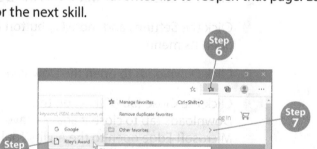

Skill Extra

Saving to the Favorites Bar

Choosing *Favorites bar* in Step 3 saves the item to the Favorites bar. When enabled, the Favorites bar appears below the Address bar in the Microsoft Edge window. To enable the Favorites bar, click the Settings and more (...) button, point to the *Favorites* command, point to the *Show favorites bar* command, and then click *Always*.

The advantage of saving an item to the Favorites bar is that the shortcut will be available as a button there, without requiring you to open the Favorites menu. The disadvantage is that there is space for only a limited number of buttons to appear on the Favorites bar at once.

Review Browser History and Clear Browsing Data

The **browser history** is a list of all the websites you have recently visited. You can use it to return to recent pages quickly, even if you did not mark them as favorites.

A **cookie** is a small text file that a website might save to your hard drive to help remember your settings when you visit the same page again. For example, a cookie might remember the content of your shopping cart or what country you are in. Some advertisers also use cookies to track your shopping and browsing habits.

For privacy, you can clear your browsing data, including history and cookies, so that nobody else using your computer can see what sites you have visited.

Review Browser History

1. With Microsoft Edge open, click the Settings and more (...) button to open a menu.

2 Another Way
Press Ctrl + H to open the History list.

2. Click the *History* command to open the History submenu.

3. Click the *Manage History* command.

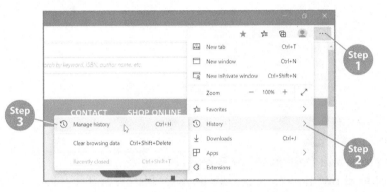

TIP

In Step 4, if you don't see *Google* in the History list, scroll down in the History list. If you still don't see it, remove some other item from the history list instead of Google.

4. Click the X to the right of *Google* to remove that item.

Clear Browsing Data

5. Click the Settings and more (…) button to open a menu.

6. On the menu, point to *History* and then click *Clear browsing data*.

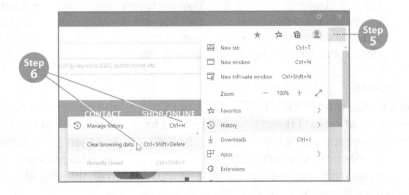

TIP

If you are using your own PC, you might not want to clear passwords and form data because it is useful to have that information fill in automatically. If you are using a public or school computer, you should clear that data to protect your privacy. If you scroll down in the Clear browsing data dialog box, you see options for clearing passwords and form data.

7 For each type of data listed, click to insert a check mark if you want to clear the data, or click to remove the check mark if you want to keep the data.

8 Click the Clear now button to remove the selected types of data. The process may take a few minutes to complete.

9 Close the Settings and History tabs. Leave Microsoft Edge open for the next skill.

Skill Extras

Clearing History and Data in Other Browsers

The table below shows how to clear your browser history and cookies in three popular browsers.

Browser	View History	Clear Browsing Data
Internet Explorer	Click the Favorites button (star) and then click *History* in the Navigation pane.	Click the Tools button (cog), point to *Safety* on the menu, and then click *Delete browsing history*. In the Delete Browsing History dialog box, click the data type check boxes to insert or remove check marks, and then click Delete to remove all selected types of data.
Mozilla Firefox	Click the View history, saved bookmarks, and more button (three vertical lines and one diagonal line), and then click *History*.	View the history (see instructions at left), and then click *Clear Recent History*. In the dialog box, click the *Time range to clear* box arrow, click the time range within which you want to clear browsing data (or click *Everything* to clear it all), and then click the Clear Now button.
Google Chrome	Click the Customize and control Google Chrome button (three vertically stacked dots), point to *History*, and then click *History*.	View the history (see instructions at left), and then click *Clear browsing data*. In the Clear browsing data dialog box, click the data type check boxes to insert or remove check marks and then click the Clear Data button to remove all selected types of data.

Blocking Cookies

A third-party cookie is one that is placed on your PC by an advertiser that doesn't directly have anything to do with the website you are visiting. You can choose to block third-party cookies in Microsoft Edge to prevent advertisers from tracking you (or at least make it more difficult for them to do so). Click the Settings and more (...) button, and then click *Settings*. In the search box at the top of the Settings pane, type cookies and then press Enter. In the search results, under Site permissions, click *Cookies and site data*. Drag the slider to enable the *Block third-party cookies* setting.

Skill 7
Print a Web Page

You can print a web page to create a hard copy of it that you can share offline with others. You can choose which printer to use, how many copies to print, and whether to print in portrait or landscape orientation. Depending on your chosen printer, you may also be able to adjust other settings.

1 With Microsoft Edge open, click in the Address bar, type https://W10.ParadigmEducation.com/Riley, and then press Enter if that page is not already displayed from the previous skill.

2-3 *Another Way*
Press Ctrl + P.

2 Click the Settings and more (…) button to open a menu.

3 Click *Print* to open the Print dialog box.

TIP

Ask your instructor which printer to use if you are not sure.

4 Click the *Printer* box and then click the desired printer in the drop-down list, if it is not already selected.

5 Click the *Portrait* or the *Landscape* option button to choose the desired page orientation.

TIP

Landscape orientation prints along the wide side of the paper; portrait prints along the narrow side. You can sometimes make a multipage print job fit on fewer sheets of paper by changing the orientation.

6 Click the Print button if you want to print the page. Otherwise, click the Cancel button.

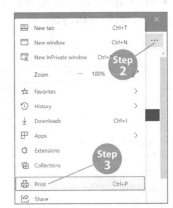

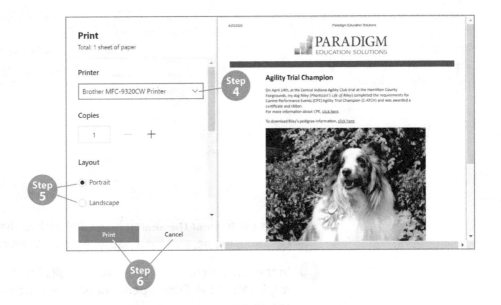

7 Close the Microsoft Edge browser window.

Skill Extra

Using More Print Settings

Before clicking the Print button in Step 6, you might want to scroll down in the left pane to access additional settings, such as *Pages*. You can also click <u>More settings</u> to investigate the settings specific to your printer. For example, you might be able to change paper size, paper source, and collation options. (*Collation* refers to the order in which the pages print when you are printing multiple copies of a multipage file.)

Use Windows Search to Get Information Online

The search box on the taskbar in Windows 10 has advanced search capabilities, and is woven tightly into almost every part of Windows 10.

- In Chapter 1, Skill 3, Search helped you find applications to run.
- In Chapter 1, Skill 7, Search served as a portal to Windows help information.
- In Chapter 2, Skill 9, Search helped you locate files and folders on your PC.

Windows Search can also help you find information on the web. It is able to process questions in natural language form, so you can phrase a question as if you were talking to a real person. You aren't limited to simple keywords like in a regular web search.

When possible, Windows Search answers within its own pane—no web browser is required. If you want to do more research on your own, or if Windows Search can't answer the question you asked directly, you can click one of the links it provides, such as a link to a Bing search.

1 On the Windows taskbar, click in the search box. Windows Search greets you with a pop-up pane.

TIP

If you press Enter in Step 2, you will go to whatever result is selected at the top of the results pane (probably the Bing search page), rather than allowing Windows Search to find the answer.

2 Type capital of Nebraska and then pause. Do not press Enter. Windows Search will report the information momentarily.

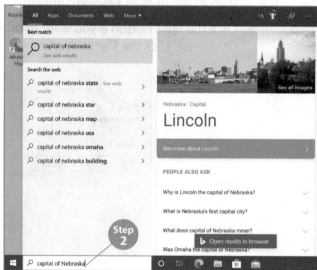

TIP

To close the Windows Search pane without opening Microsoft Edge, click away from the pane.

3 Press Esc to clear the search box, click back in the search box again, type tuna casserole recipe, and then pause. Again, do not press Enter.

4 In the top left corner of the search results list, click tuna casserole recipe See web results. Microsoft Edge opens and shows search results for that topic using the Bing search engine.

5 Close the Microsoft Edge browser window.

Skill Extra

Using Voice Commands with Cortana

If your computer has a microphone, you can perform searches via voice commands using **Cortana**, the voice-controlled personal assistant in Windows. Just click the Talk to Cortana button (the circle) to the right of the search box on the Windows taskbar to activate the voice feature and then speak clearly into your microphone. The first time you click the Talk to Cortana button, Windows walks you through a brief setup process.

Tasks Summary

Task	Button/Icon/Option	Action
clear an item from browsing history	☒	Click Settings and more (...) button, point to *History*, click *Manage history*, click X for item to delete it.
close browser tab	☒	In Microsoft Edge browser, click Close button on tab.
duplicate browser tab	Duplicate tab	In Microsoft Edge browser, right-click tab, click *Duplicate tab*.
go back, go forward, or refresh web page	← → ↻	On Address bar in Microsoft Edge browser, click Back, Forward, or Refresh button.
go to a URL	⊕ http://paradigmeducation.com	In Microsoft Edge browser, click in Address bar, type address, press Enter.
open and close Favorites	☆☰	On Address bar in Microsoft Edge browser, click Favorites button to open Favorites menu. Click away from the menu or press Esc to close it.
open and close Downloads list	↓ Downloads	Click Settings and more (...) button and click *Downloads* to open list on a new tab.
open new browser tab	+	In Microsoft Edge browser, click the New tab button.
print web page	🖶 Print	On web page in Microsoft Edge browser, click Settings and more (...) button, click *Print*, choose settings, click Print button.
save and name favorite	☆	On web page in Microsoft Edge browser, click Add this page to favorites button (star with plus sign), edit text in *Name* box, choose a location from Folder list box, click Done button.
search web using Bing default search engine	⌕ Search or enter web address	In Microsoft Edge browser, click in Address bar or search box, type search term or phrase, press Enter, click search result.
search web using another search engine		In Microsoft Edge browser, navigate to search engine home page, type search term or phrase in search box, press Enter if needed, click search result.
start Microsoft Edge browser	🌀	On Windows taskbar, click Microsoft Edge button.
use Windows Search to get information online	⌕ Type here to search	On Windows taskbar, click in search box, type search term or phrase and pause, click result.
view browsing history	↻ History	Click Settings and more (...) button, point to *History*, review items on Recently closed list or click *Manage history* to see more.

Chapter 4

The online course includes additional training and assessment resources.

Using OneDrive and Office for the Web

In this chapter, you will learn how to use the web-based OneDrive interface to store, access, and manage files in OneDrive.

OneDrive is a Microsoft-provided cloud storage system. A *cloud storage system* is a secure online storage location that users can access from any computing device that has internet access. Each Microsoft account has a certain amount of free storage space in OneDrive, and users can purchase additional space as needed. Many people use OneDrive to store personal files that they need to access from multiple devices. They can also share OneDrive files and folders with other online users.

Microsoft provides free web-based business productivity applications, called Office for the web applications. These are simplified versions of the popular Microsoft 365 desktop applications, including Word, Excel, PowerPoint, and OneNote. The web-based applications enable people to access Microsoft 365 data files even when using a computer that does not have the full desktop version of the application installed. When you use these web-based apps, the default storage location is OneDrive.

The web-based applications have all the features that most people need for everyday projects. The corresponding desktop applications offer more advanced and specialized features. For example, the desktop version of Microsoft Word offers features for creating indexes and bibliographies, features not found in Word for the web.

Skills You Learn

1 Use File Explorer to Access OneDrive and Upload Student Data Files
2 Sign In to and Out of OneDrive.com
3 Navigate between Folders and Create a New Folder
4 Upload Files
5 Create a New File in an Office for the Web App
6 Edit a File in an Office for the Web App
7 Edit a File in a Microsoft 365 Application
8 Share a Folder from OneDrive

Files You Use

Before beginning this chapter, make sure you have copied the W10-StudentDataFiles folder to your USB flash drive (see Chapter 2, Skill 4, page 24). In the skills for this chapter, you will learn how to upload the entire folder to OneDrive and will use the data files listed here.

W10-C4-Birthdays.txt
W10-C4-Mortgage.xlsx

Skill 1
Use File Explorer to Access OneDrive and Upload Student Data Files

Each Microsoft account has its own separate OneDrive storage. When you sign in to Windows 10 with your Microsoft account, Windows connects to the OneDrive server so you can access your OneDrive content via File Explorer. File Explorer includes a shortcut to OneDrive in the Navigation pane.

By default, Windows will *sync* OneDrive content to a folder on the local hard drive. In other words, Windows will keep a copy of everything from your OneDrive in a special user folder on your hard drive. This means that if the internet is not available, you still have access to your content. This folder is stored in your user folders (C: > Users > *username* > OneDrive).

When you work with OneDrive content on your local PC, you are technically working with local copies of content, not the online versions. However, the online versions are immediately synchronized to match the local versions whenever internet access is available. You can therefore upload files and folders to OneDrive by placing them in your OneDrive folder in File Explorer. If your PC is not connected to the internet, the synchronization automatically occurs whenever internet connectivity becomes available.

TIP

You downloaded the student data files to a USB flash drive in Chapter 2, Skill 4.

TIP

If at any point a Set Up OneDrive window appears, work through it to ensure you are signed in with your Microsoft account.

TIP

In Step 3, you may need to scroll down to find the USB flash drive in the Navigation pane.

1 Connect the USB flash drive containing the student data files for this course to your computer.

2 On the Windows taskbar, click the File Explorer button.

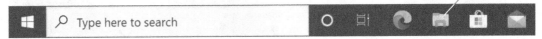

3 In the Navigation pane, click the USB flash drive to display its contents.

4 In the file list pane, click the *W10-StudentDataFiles* folder and then press Ctrl + C to copy it to the Clipboard.

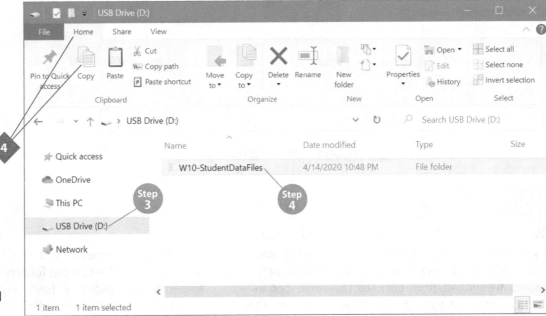

4 *Another Way*
Click the *W10-StudentDataFiles* folder, click the Home tab, and then click the Copy button in the Clipboard group.
OR
Right-click the *W10-StudentDataFiles* folder and then click *Copy*.

TIP

The contents of your OneDrive account may not match the contents shown here and may show different icons and statuses.

TIP

The icons you see in the *Status* column may be different. The Available when online icon appears when the content exists only online. When you open or edit a file on your local PC, it creates a locally mirrored copy and the icon changes to Available on this device. See the Skill Extra below to learn how to choose which files and folders are available locally.

⑥ **Another Way**
Right-click a blank area of the file list pane and then click *Paste*.
OR
Click the Home tab and then click the Paste button in the Clipboard group.

TIP

When you paste the copied folder in Step 6, the status icon appears briefly as a Sync pending icon while the upload to the cloud occurs and changes to a Locally available icon when it finishes.

⑤ In the Navigation pane, click *OneDrive*. Your OneDrive files (if any) and folders appear in the file list pane.

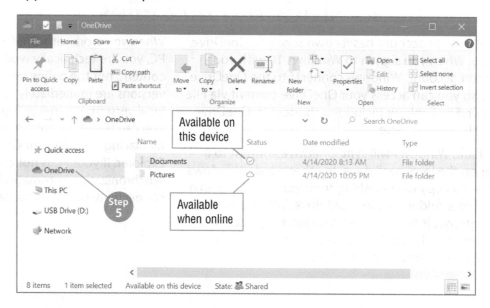

⑥ Press Ctrl + V to paste the copied folder into your OneDrive folder.

⑦ Click the Close (X) button to close the File Explorer window.

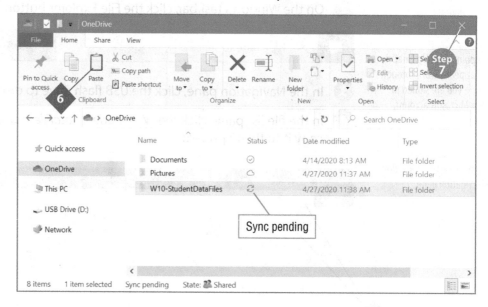

⑧ Disconnect the USB flash drive.

Skill Extra

Choosing Which Folders to Keep Synchronized

If you have a lot of content on your OneDrive, you might prefer not to sync all of it. To choose which folders are synced, right-click the OneDrive icon in the notification area of the Windows taskbar and then click *Settings*. (You might need to click the up arrow in the notification area to see the OneDrive icon.) In the

Microsoft OneDrive dialog box, click the Account tab and then click the Choose folders button. In the Choose folders screen, click the check boxes to indicate how you want OneDrive to handle each folder. Click OK and then click OK again when you are finished.

Skill 2
Sign In to and Out of OneDrive.com

As you saw in Skill 1, you can work with OneDrive in a basic way through File Explorer. The online interface at OneDrive.com, however, provides even more capabilities. For example, using the online interface, you can create new documents using Office for the web applications. The rest of this chapter assumes you are using the online version of OneDrive.

You can access OneDrive.com from any web browser. In this chapter you will use the Microsoft Edge browser, which is the default browser in Windows 10. You read about Microsoft Edge in Chapter 3.

1. On the Windows taskbar, click the Microsoft Edge button to open the browser window.

2. Type onedrive.com in the Address bar and then press Enter. If a *Files* section appears, you are already signed in, and you can skip to Step 8.

3. If you see an introductory page with a Sign in button, click the Sign in button.

TIP

If you have previously signed out during this browser session, you might not see the prompts in Steps 3–5, or the Sign in dialog box may appear somewhat different.

4. At the Sign in prompt, type the email address associated with your Microsoft account.

5. Click the Next button.

TIP

Microsoft periodically changes the OneDrive web interface, so the sign-in procedure you encounter might differ slightly from the one described here.

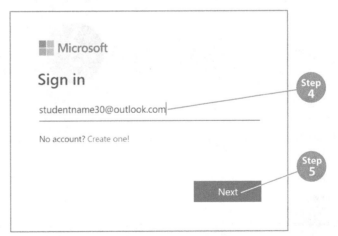

6 In the *Password* text box, type your Microsoft account password.

7 Click the Sign in button.

8 Click the Account manager button in the upper right corner of the OneDrive.com page. A menu appears.

9 Click *Sign out*.

10 Click the Close (X) button to close the Microsoft Edge browser window.

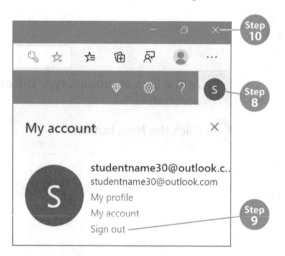

Skill Extras

Customizing the User Icon

By default, the Account manager button is a plain circle with the first letter of your name in it, as shown in the screen capture for Step 8 of this skill. To change it to your own photo, click the Account manager button, click *My profile*, click *Add a picture*, and then follow the prompts to add a picture. The same picture will appear in all your Microsoft applications.

Staying Signed In

You might see a *Keep me signed in* check box below the *Password* box when you sign in. If that appears, you can click the check box to insert a check mark to stay signed in between sessions.

Skill 3

Navigate between Folders and Create a New Folder

After you sign in to OneDrive.com, you see folders in the file list pane on the right. If OneDrive opens in Tiles view, the folders appear as large tiles; if it opens in List view, you see a list of small folders with names, dates modified, and other details. There are two other views as well: Compact list and Photo. You might also see some files if you have previously used OneDrive with this Microsoft account.

As in File Explorer, the interface at OneDrive.com contains a Navigation pane on the left. If you don't see the Navigation pane, widen the browser window to make it appear.

The Navigation pane has the following links:

- *My files* is the OneDrive equivalent of *This PC* on your local PC. You can click *My files* at any time to come back to the top level of your OneDrive.

- *Recent* opens a list of data files that you have recently opened from OneDrive, if any, regardless of the folder they are in.
- *Photos* opens a list of photos stored on your OneDrive, regardless of the folder they are in.
- *Shared* opens a list of shortcuts to folders and files that either you have shared or someone else has shared with you.
- *Recycle bin* opens a list of files you have deleted from OneDrive.

You might also see a *PCs* link if your Microsoft account is set up on multiple computers.

The default folders include Documents, Pictures, Personal Vault, and sometimes Music. You can use the default folders, create your own folders, or copy folders from your local PC to OneDrive. In this skill, you learn to create a folder and name it.

TIP

You copied the W10-StudentDataFiles folder to OneDrive in Skill 1. If it does not appear immediately in Step 1, wait a few minutes for your PC and OneDrive.com to sync.

TIP

At OneDrive.com, clicking an item opens it; in File Explorer, clicking an item selects it and double-clicking opens it.

1. Open Microsoft Edge, go to OneDrive.com, and sign in to your account using the steps in Skill 2.

2. With *My files* selected in the Navigation pane, click the *W10-StudentDataFiles* folder in the file list pane to open the folder.

If the Navigation pane doesn't display, widen the browser window.

Click the View options button and then click *Tiles* if the folders do not display as shown here in Step 2.

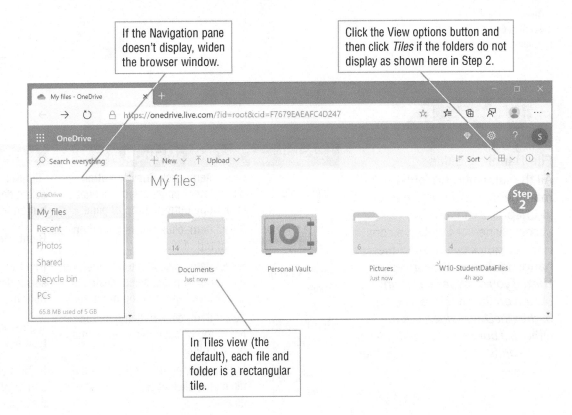

In Tiles view (the default), each file and folder is a rectangular tile.

TIP

In List view, clicking or double-clicking the name of an item opens the item, and clicking the date modified or size selects the item.

3 In the upper right corner of the file list pane, click the Open the view options menu button and then click *List*. Notice that the display changes to show the folders in List view.

4 Click the Back button in the browser window to return to the previous location.

4 Another Way
Click *My files* in the Navigation pane to return to the top level of the OneDrive folder structure.

5 Another Way
Right-click a blank area above or below the file list, click *New*, and then click *Folder*.

5 On the bar at the top of the page, click the New button.

6 Click *Folder* in the drop-down list.

TIP

Notice that the view you choose with the View options button applies to all locations in OneDrive.

7 In the Folder dialog box, type W10-C4-Miscellaneous in the *Folder* box.

8 Click the Create button. The new folder appears in the file list pane. Leave Microsoft Edge open at OneDrive.com for the next skill.

TIP

After Step 8, small blue lines show around the upper left corner of the new **W10-C4-Miscellaneous** file. These blue lines indicate an item is new.

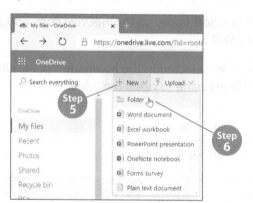

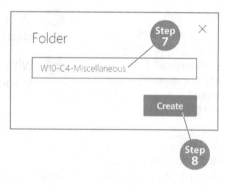

Skill Extra

Using Other File-Handling Skills

All the same file and folder management skills you learned in Chapter 2 can also be accomplished at OneDrive.com. Here's a quick overview of file-handling skills in OneDrive. *Hint: If you don't see a certain button on the bar across the top of the OneDrive page, click the Other (...) button to see undisplayed commands, or widen your browser window.*

Skill	Method	Alternative Method
Copy a file	Select item, click Copy to button on bar at top of page, select destination, click Copy button at top of pane.	Right-click item, click *Copy to*, select destination, click Copy button at top of pane.
Delete a file or folder	Select item, click Delete button on bar at top of page.	Right-click item, click *Delete*.
Move a file or folder	Select item, click Move to button on bar at top of page, select destination, click Move button at top of pane.	Right-click item, click *Move to*, select destination, click Move button at top of pane.
Rename a file or folder	Select item, click Rename button on bar at top of page, type new name, press Enter.	Right-click item, click *Rename*, type new name, press Enter.
Select a file or folder	In List view, point to the left of the file name, click check circle that appears.	In Tiles view, point to upper right corner of tile, click check circle that appears.

Skill 4
Upload Files

Copying files from your local PC to an online storage location such as OneDrive is called *uploading*. Uploading is the opposite of *downloading*, which means copying an item from an online storage location to your local PC. Note that uploading and downloading make copies of files; they do not move the original files.

You might upload a file so that it will be available when you use a different computer, or in preparation for sharing the file online with others (covered in Skill 8).

Uploading via OneDrive.com has the same end result as uploading via File Explorer (covered in Skill 1). The OneDrive.com method works directly with the online storage location, however, whereas File Explorer interacts with the copy on your hard drive. As a result, uploads performed via OneDrive.com are immediate, whereas uploads performed with File Explorer may take a few minutes to synchronize.

1. Connect the USB flash drive containing the student data files to your computer.

2. With Microsoft Edge open to the My files screen in your OneDrive.com account, click the Upload button and then click *Files*.

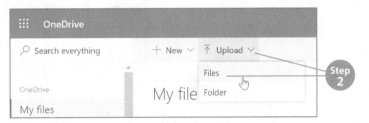

3. In the Navigation pane of the Open dialog box, click the USB flash drive where your downloaded student data files are stored, navigate to the W10-Chapter4 folder on your flash drive, and then click **W10-C4-Birthdays** to select it.

4. Press and hold the Shift key, click **W10-C4-Mortgage**, and then release the Shift key. Both files will be selected.

5. Click the Open button. Wait for the files to finish uploading and appear in the file list pane.

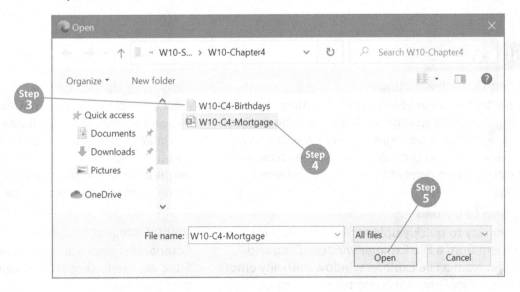

TIP

If your file list pane does not match the one shown here, you are not in List view. Click the Open the view options button in the upper right corner of the page and then click *List* to switch to List view if needed.

7 ▶ **Another Way**

If you can't see both the files and the destination folder at once without scrolling, use the Move To method instead, described in the table at the bottom of page 56.

6 In the My files pane, point to the left of each file you just uploaded, and then click the check circles that appear to insert check marks and select the files.

7 Drag the selected files and drop them on the W10-C4-Miscellaneous folder to move them there. Leave Microsoft Edge open to your file list pane at OneDrive.com for the next skill.

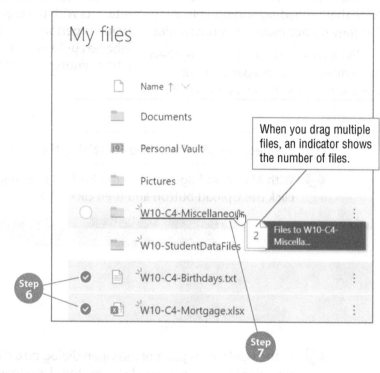

My files

Name ↑ ∨

Documents

Personal Vault

Pictures

W10-C4-Miscellaneous

W10-StudentDataFiles

When you drag multiple files, an indicator shows the number of files.

2 Files to W10-C4-Miscella...

Step 6

✓ W10-C4-Birthdays.txt

✓ W10-C4-Mortgage.xlsx

Step 7

Skill Extras

Viewing OneDrive Settings

To view and manage your OneDrive settings, including the amount of file storage available, click the Settings icon (⚙) in the upper right corner of the OneDrive web page and then click *Options*. Use the commands in the Navigation pane at the left to see different settings.

Dragging to Upload

Another way to quickly upload files or folders is to drag them from a File Explorer window. Drag-and-drop files from a File Explorer window onto any empty area of the OneDrive file listing to copy them to OneDrive.

Resolving Upload Errors

After you upload files to OneDrive, an Error icon (⊘) appears above the file list if one or more files did not upload correctly. Click this icon to see a list of errors, and then click an action to resolve an error. An error might occur if you try to upload a file with the same name as an existing file. You can choose to keep both files, or to replace the existing file with the new one.

Using Compact List View

Compact list view is similar to List view, except the items listed are more compact; you can use it if you prefer it over List view.

Skill 5
Create a New File in an Office for the Web App

From OneDrive.com, you can access several Office for the web applications. These are simplified versions of the corresponding Microsoft 365 desktop applications, including Word, Excel, PowerPoint, and OneNote. These web applications offer a convenient way of creating and editing Microsoft 365 or Microsoft Office compatible content even if you are using a computer that does not have the full desktop version installed. When you create a new file using one of the Office for the web apps, OneDrive saves your work automatically. The steps provided here use Word as an example, but they also work in most of the other Office for the web apps too.

TIP

When creating a new file, start by selecting the location to store it—in this case, the top folder level of your OneDrive.

1. With Microsoft Edge open to the file list pane in your OneDrive.com account, click *My files* in the Navigation pane to ensure you are starting at the top folder level.

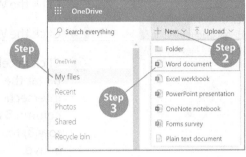

2. On the bar at the top of the page, click the New button.

TIP

The first time you open Word for the web, a window might open with video instructions. Close the video window.

3. Click *Word document* in the drop-down list.

4. In the new Word document that opens, type your full name and then press Enter.

5. Type your school name and then triple-click the school name to select it.

TIP

The Home tab contains commands for formatting text, including character formatting like bold, italic, and underline.

6. Click the Home tab on the ribbon if needed, and then click the Bold button.

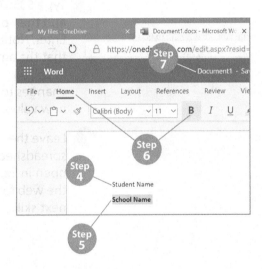

7. In the blue bar at the top of the page, click the name of the file you are working in. It will be a generic name, such as *Document1*. A *File Name* text box appears.

8. In the *File Name* text box, type W10-C4-School and then press Enter to rename the file.

9. In the upper left corner, click the App launcher button to open a Microsoft 365 menu and then click the OneDrive button.

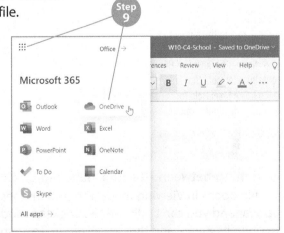

🔟 **Another Way**

If you cannot see the file and the destination folder at once, use the move skill instead, as described at the bottom of page 56.

10. In the file list pane, drag the **W10-C4-School** file to the W10-C4-Miscellaneous folder and drop it there. The file moves to that folder. Leave Microsoft Edge open to your file list pane at OneDrive.com for the next skill.

Skill 6
Edit a File in an Office for the Web App

At OneDrive.com, it is easy to open and edit a data file that is supported by an Office for the web app. Simply click the file, and it opens in the appropriate app. For example, if you click a Word document, it opens in Word for the web. If you click a file that is not supported by an Office for the web app, OneDrive downloads the file to your local hard drive and then offers you an Open button. This allows you to try to open the file using the applications installed on your PC.

1 With Microsoft Edge open to your OneDrive.com account, click *My files* in the Navigation pane to ensure you are starting at the top folder level.

TIP
You created the W10-C4-Miscellaneous folder in Skill 3 and added files to it in Skills 4 and 5.

2 Click the W10-C4-Miscellaneous folder link to view the folder's content.

3 Click the W10-C4-Mortgage.xlsx file link to open the file in Excel for the web.

4 Click in cell B3 (at the intersection of column B and row 3) to make it active.

TIP
If the ribbon does not appear and you are not able to edit the file in Step 5, see the Skill Extra following these steps.

5 Type $350,000 and then press Enter. Notice that the amount in cell B3 changes to the new value.

6 Leave the spreadsheet open in Excel for the web for the next skill.

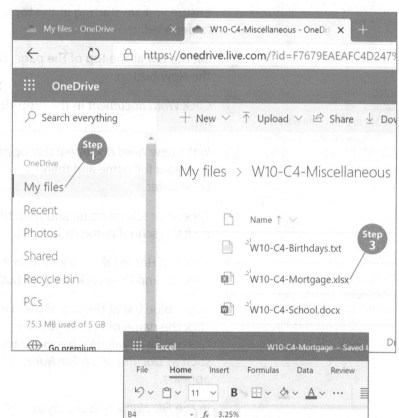

TIP
After changing the amount in cell B3, the amount in cell B6 also changes because cell B6 contains a formula that links to cell B3. See Excel Help for information about formulas.

Skill Extra

Switching between Reading View and Editing View

If a file opens in Viewing mode, the ribbon doesn't appear and you can't edit the file. Click the Mode button to open its menu, and then click *Editing*. To change back to Viewing mode, click the View tab and then click the Mode button again to reopen its menu and then click *Viewing*.

Skill 7
Edit a File in a Microsoft 365 Application

Microsoft 365 applications are full-featured versions of the Office applications. Because they are desktop applications installed to a local drive as opposed to the cloud, you can use them even when not connected to the internet. If your computer has Microsoft 365 applications installed, you might prefer to use them to create and edit files.

You can open a Microsoft 365 application from the OneDrive web interface, or you can open one from the Start menu or from File Explorer without going through a web browser. Because OneDrive syncs your stored files on the local PC and online, you can access your saved files from either location.

TIP

Microsoft periodically changes the web-based apps, and they don't all work the same way.

Instead of an Open in Desktop App button in Step 1, some apps have a Mode button, which is set to Editing mode by default. You can click the Mode button to open a menu and then click Open in Desktop App.

1. With Microsoft Edge still open to Excel for the web from the previous skill, click the Open in Desktop App button.

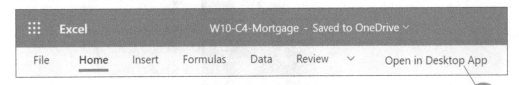

2. If you see a confirmation message, click the Open button.

3. In the desktop version of Excel, click in cell B5 (at the intersection of column B and row 5) to make it active.

4. Type 15 and then press Enter. Notice that the amount in cell B5 changes to reflect the new term, and the amount in cell B6 changes because the payment is recalculated.

5. Click the Close (X) button in the Excel window to close the application.

TIP

OneDrive files are saved automatically. If you had been editing a file stored only on a local disk, you would have been prompted to save your work before Excel closed.

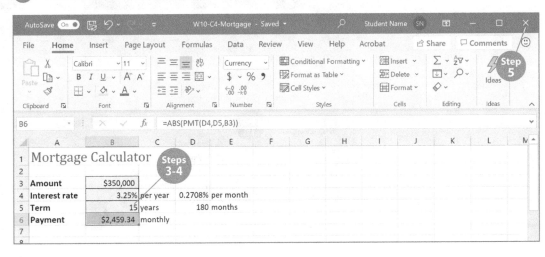

6. If needed, click the Microsoft Edge button on the Windows taskbar to return to Microsoft Edge.

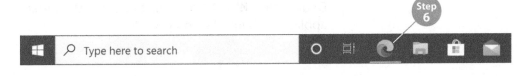

7. If an All done dialog box appears in Microsoft Edge, click the Resume editing here button. Notice that the changes you made in Step 4 are already reflected in the worksheet in Excel for the web.

8. Click the Close (X) button for the W10-C4-Mortgage.xlsx tab to close Excel for the web.

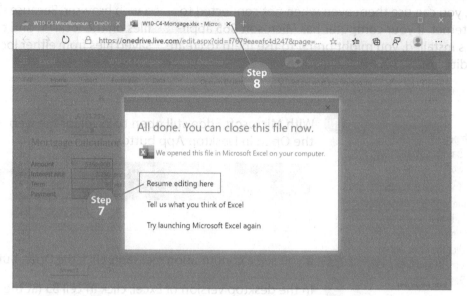

9. On the Windows taskbar, click the File Explorer button to open File Explorer.

10. In the Navigation pane, click *OneDrive*.

11. Double-click **W10-C4-Miscellaneous**.

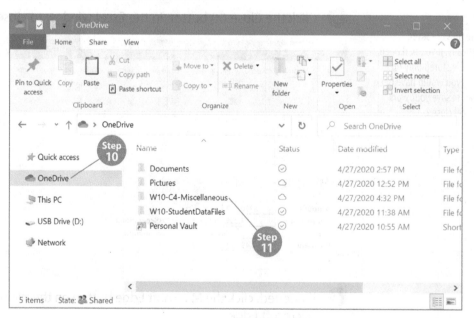

12. Double-click **W10-C4-School**. It opens in the desktop version of Word, if that application is installed on your PC.

13 In Word, triple-click your name to select it.

14 Click the Italic button in the Paragraph group to italicize your selected name.

TIP

In Step 16, if you are prompted to choose which OneDrive account to save to, click the one associated with your Microsoft account.

15 On the Quick Access Toolbar on the title bar, click the Undo button to undo the change.

16 If AutoSave is set to *Off*, click it to change it to *On*.

17 Click the Close (X) button in the Word window to close it.

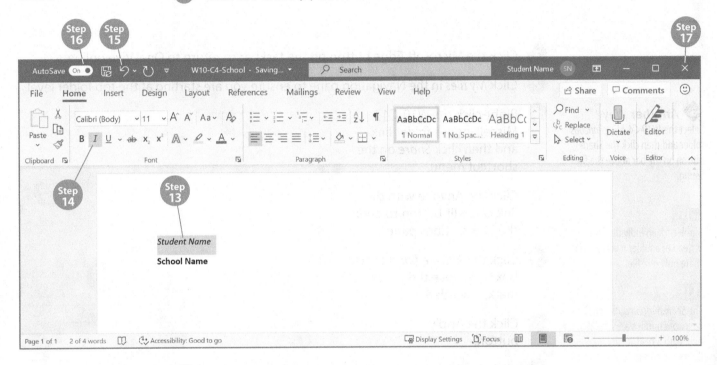

18 Click the Close (X) button to close File Explorer.

Skill Extra

Controlling Syncing with OneDrive

Notice that in Step 11, a cloud icon appears next to the W10-C4-Miscellaneous file in File Explorer. That means this folder is stored online and there is currently no local copy of it. It is accessible only when you are connected to the internet. You could right-click the file name and choose *Always keep on this device* to set its contents to be downloaded to the local PC whenever the device connects to the internet. OneDrive gives you this choice so you don't have to always sync the content in both locations and so that OneDrive files don't take up too much room on your local PC.

To manage the synchronization settings, you can right-click the OneDrive icon (☁) in the notification area on the right side of the Windows taskbar and choose *Settings*. (You might have to click *Show hidden icons* to see the OneDrive icon in the notification area.) In the dialog box that appears, click the Settings tab. Click the *Save space and download files as you use them* check box to insert a check mark. When the check box is marked, files created online are not automatically downloaded to this device; when the check box does not contain a check mark, they are. Click OK to close the dialog box.

Skill 8

Share a Folder from OneDrive

You can share your OneDrive content with other people, whether they are in the same office or halfway around the world. You can allow others to edit the files, or you can restrict access so they can only view the files (also called *read-only access*). If someone has the link to the folder, they can use that link to access the folder in any web browser. Users with read-only access to a shared file or folder may download it and make changes to their own copy.

You can share individual files or entire folders. Sharing a folder simplifies the process of sharing multiple files because anything you later place inside that folder will be shared with the same permissions as the folder itself.

1 Click the Microsoft Edge button on the taskbar to return to OneDrive online.

2 Click *My files* in the Navigation pane to ensure you are starting at the top folder level.

3 **Another Way**
Select the *W10-C4-Miscellaneous* folder and then click the Share button on the bar above the file listing.

3 Right-click the <u>W10-C4-Miscellaneous</u> folder link and then click *Share* on the shortcut menu.

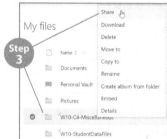

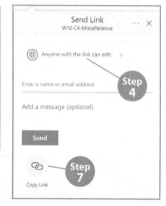

4 Click the Anyone with the link can edit button to open the Link settings pane.

TIP
Right-click an individual file instead of a folder if you want to share only one file.

5 Click the *Allow editing* check box to remove the check mark, if needed.

TIP
The *Set expiration date* and *Set password* options are available only with a paid version of OneDrive; you will not need these options for this book.

6 Click the Apply button.

7 Click the Copy Link button to copy the link to the Clipboard. From the Clipboard, you could paste this link anywhere, such as in an email or a social media post.

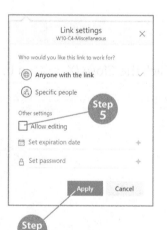

TIP
To stop sharing a folder, right click it, click *Share*, More options (...) button, and then *Manage Access*. In the Manage Access pane, click the X next to the the link that you want to stop sharing. In the Remove link dialog box, confirm your choice by clicking *Remove link*.

8 Click the Close (X) button in the pane to close it.

9 In the Navigation pane, click *Shared*. Notice that the W10-C4-Miscellaneous folder appears under the *Shared by me* heading in the file list pane.

10 Sign out of OneDrive.com and then close the browser window.

Skill Extra

Finding a Link Address Again

Any time you need to get the link for a shared folder, you can easily retrieve it. Select the shared folder in the file list pane and then click the Open the details pane button (⊙) on the toolbar. Click *Manage access* for access to the link.

Tasks Summary

Task	Button/Icon/Option	Action
access OneDrive using File Explorer	☁ OneDrive	In Navigation pane of File Explorer window, click *OneDrive*.
change views at OneDrive.com	▦ ≡	On bar at top of page, click Open the view options menu button.
close Office for the web file at OneDrive.com	✕	Click Close button for the browser tab containing the open file.
copy selected file or folder at OneDrive.com	🗐 Copy to	On bar at top of page, click Copy to button, select destination, click Copy button at top of pane.
copy selected files or folders into OneDrive using File Explorer	Copy Paste	In File Explorer window, copy desired item(s), click *OneDrive* in Navigation pane, open desired OneDrive folder in file list pane, paste item(s) into folder.
create and name new document at OneDrive.com	+ New ⌄	On bar at top of page, click New button, click desired file type in drop-down list.
create and name new folder at OneDrive.com	📁 Folder	Navigate to desired folder location, click New button on bar at top of page, click *Folder*, type name, click Create button.
delete file or folder at OneDrive.com	🗑 Delete	In file list pane, select item, click Delete button on bar at top of page.
edit file in Office for the web app at OneDrive.com	▦ W10-C4-Mortgage.xlsx	In file list pane, click file.
move file or folder at OneDrive.com	⊞ Move to	In file list pane, select item, click Move to button on bar at top of page, select destination, click Move button at top of pane.
move files using drag-and-drop at OneDrive.com		In file list pane, select files, drag files, drop files on destination.
navigate to folder at OneDrive.com	My files	In Navigation pane, click *My files*, click desired folder.
open a file from Excel for the web in Excel 365	Open in Desktop App	On the bar at the top, click Open in Desktop App button, click Open button.
rename file or folder at OneDrive.com	✎ Rename	In file list pane, select item, click More button on bar at top of page if needed, click *Rename*, type new name, press Enter.
return to OneDrive from Office for the web app	⣿ ☁ OneDrive	In Office for the web document tab in browser, click App launcher button and click OneDrive.
select file or folder at OneDrive.com	⊘	In List view, point to left of file name, click check circle. In Tiles view, point to upper right corner of tile, click check circle.
share file or folder at OneDrive.com	↪ Share	In file list pane, right-click file or folder, click *Share*, click Copy link button, click Copy button, paste link where desired.
sign in to OneDrive.com		At introductory page, click Sign in button, type Microsoft account email address, click Next, type password, click Sign in button.
sign out of OneDrive.com	Sign out	On bar at top of page, click the Account manager button, click *Sign out*.
upload files at OneDrive.com	↑ Upload	On bar at top of page, click Upload button, navigate to files, select files, click Open button.

Chapter 5

Taking Screenshots and Using OneNote

In this chapter, you will learn how to create a graphic file of what you see on your computer screen and send that file to others via email. This type of graphic is commonly called a *screenshot* or *screen capture*. You might need to create and email screenshots for a computer applications class. For example, your instructor might ask you to take a screenshot to show you have completed a certain exercise. You might also find it useful to take screenshots for your own reference or to share with a friend. There are several ways to create these, including using the Print Screen key to take Windows screen captures and using the Snip & Sketch tool in Windows.

This chapter also covers *OneNote for Windows 10*, an application that stores and organizes content from many different sources in one easy-to-access place. You might use OneNote to organize the research you gather for a report or to share your research findings with a group of classmates or coworkers.

Skills You Learn

1 Capture an Image of the Entire Screen

2 Use Snip & Sketch to Capture a Portion of the Screen

3 Email an Image Using Snip & Sketch

4 Create a Notebook, Sections, and Pages in OneNote

5 Add Content to a Page in OneNote

6 Collect and Organize Online Content in OneNote

7 Email a Link to OneNote Content

Files You Use

Before beginning this chapter, make sure you have copied the W10-StudentDataFiles folder to your USB flash drive (see Chapter 2, Skill 4, page 24). In this chapter, you will use the W10-C5-Duncan.jpg data file.

Capture an Image of the Entire Screen

The most basic way to take a screenshot is to press the Print Screen key on your keyboard. (Depending on your keyboard, you may need to press a combination of keys such as Fn + PrScn or Shift + PrScn.) This command copies an image of the entire screen to the Windows Clipboard, which you read about in Chapter 2. You can then paste the image into some other application. For example, you can paste it into a graphics program like Paint, or a word processing program like Word or WordPad.

If you want to save the captured image as a graphic file without having to paste it into a particular program, you can press the Windows logo key as you press the Print Screen key. This will capture the entire screen, place a copy on the Clipboard, and also save the graphic as a PNG file in a Screenshots folder within your Pictures folder.

---

1 ▶ Another Way
Right-click the Start button and then click *File Explorer* on the Start menu.

Pressing Windows + Print Screen in Step 2 saves the screenshot on the Clipboard and also as a PNG file on your computer.

TIP

On some keyboards, you must also press and hold the Fn key in Step 2.

TIP

If you don't see *Pictures* in Step 3, click *This PC* in the Navigation pane and then click *Pictures* below it.

1 On the Windows taskbar, click the File Explorer button.

2 Press the Windows logo key (⊞) and hold it down while you press and then release the Print Screen key. The screen dims briefly and then returns to normal.

3 In the file list pane, double-click the *Pictures* folder to open it.

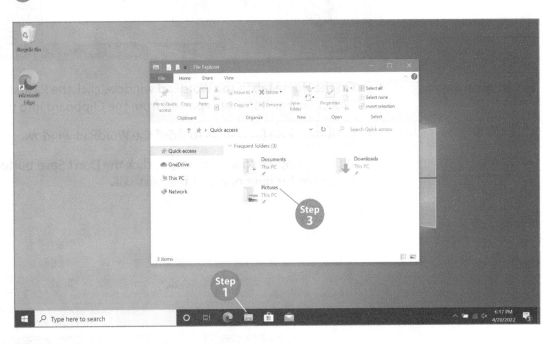

TIP

Captured screenshot files are named *Screenshot* with a number in parentheses, such as *Screenshot (1)*.

4 Double-click the *Screenshots* folder to open it. Notice that your captured screenshot file is stored here.

Skill Extra

Saving Screen Captures in a Different File Format

If you want to save a screenshot in a format other than PNG, press the Print Screen key to capture the screen. (Pressing Print Screen by itself saves the screenshot only on the Clipboard, not on your computer.) Open the Paint application, paste the image into the Paint window (Ctrl + V), click the File tab, click *Save As*, and then click the *Save as type* box arrow to choose a different file type. The choices available include *JPEG (.jpg)*, *GIF (.gif)*, *TIFF (.tif)*, *PNG (.png)*, and several types of *Bitmap (.bmp)*. Other graphics applications such as GIMP, Photoshop, and PaintShop Pro offer even more file format choices.

5-6 *Another Way*
Click the Cortana button on the Windows taskbar, click the microphone icon, and then say "Open WordPad" into the PC's microphone.

TIP

If you have never used the microphone in Windows 10 before, you are prompted to complete a short setup process the first time you click the microphone icon.

5 Click in the search box on the Windows taskbar and then type wordpad.

6 In the search results, click *WordPad App* to open a new, blank document.

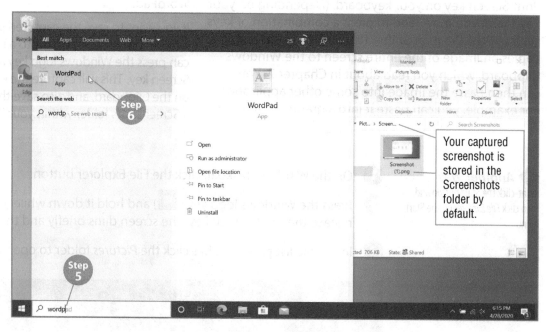

Your captured screenshot is stored in the Screenshots folder by default.

7 *Another Way*
Press Ctrl + V.

7 On the Home tab in the WordPad window, click the Paste button in the Clipboard group. Your screenshot is pasted from the Clipboard into the WordPad document.

8 Click the Close (X) button to close the WordPad window.

9 When prompted to save changes, click the Don't Save button.
Leave File Explorer open for the next skill.

Skill 2
Use Snip & Sketch to Capture a Portion of the Screen

Sometimes you might want to capture only part of a screen—such as a single dialog box or one corner of an open window. One way to achieve that result is to capture the entire screen, open the captured screenshot in a picture editing program such as Paint, and then crop the image. However, there is an easier way: use the Snip & Sketch application.

You can use the *Snip & Sketch* application to capture a part of the screen, copy the image to the Clipboard, and then paste the image anywhere you like. You can also save the image as a file or send it in an email as part of the message body or as an attachment.

1. With File Explorer open, connect the USB flash drive containing the W10-StudentDataFiles folder to your PC.

2. On the Windows taskbar, type snip in the search box.

3. In the search results, click *Snip & Sketch App* to open the Snip & Sketch application.

TIP

On some devices, the Snip & Sketch application may not be listed under the *Best match* section, so be sure to locate Snip & Sketch in the search results list.

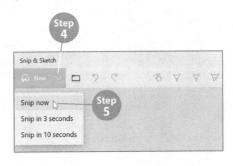

4. Click the New button arrow to open a menu.

5. On the menu, click *Snip now*. A toolbar appears across the top of the desktop.

TIP

The New button may appear at the top of the screen as shown here, or at the bottom left, depending on the window size.

TIP

The toolbar offers four options: *Rectangular Snip* (define a rectangular area), *Freeform Snip* (drag to define a freeform area), *Window Snip* (select an open window), and *Fullscreen Snip* (capture the full screen).

6 Click the Window Snip button on the toolbar.

7 Hover the mouse pointer over the File Explorer window. That window appears bright and the rest of the screen appears dimmer.

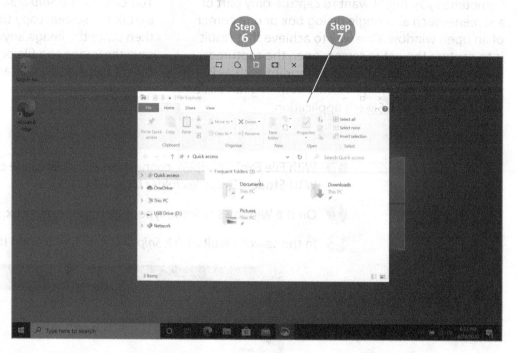

8 Click the File Explorer window to capture that window. The screen capture appears in the Snip & Sketch window.

9 Another Way
In Step 9, you can also use the Ctrl + C keyboard shortcut to copy the image to the Windows Clipboard.

9 On the Snip & Sketch toolbar, click the Copy button to copy the image to the Windows Clipboard.

10 Click the Save as button to open the Save As dialog box.

TIP

The Copy button may be at the top right as shown here, or at the bottom right, depending on the window size.

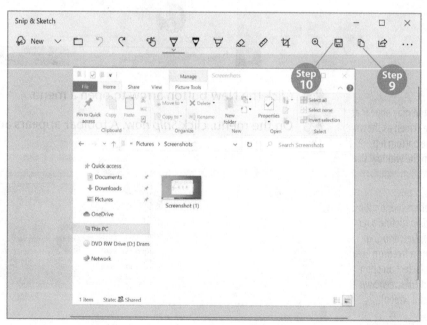

TIP

The W10-Chapter5 folder
is located in your
W10-StudentDataFiles folder.

11 In the Save As dialog box, navigate to the W10-Chapter5 folder on your USB flash drive.

12 In the *File name* text box, type W10-C5-S2-Snip to replace the default file name.

13 If the *Save as* type is not set to *PNG*, click to open the *Save as type* drop-down list and then click *PNG*.

14 Click the Save button to save the snip as a new file. Leave the Snip & Sketch application window open and your USB flash drive connected for the next skill.

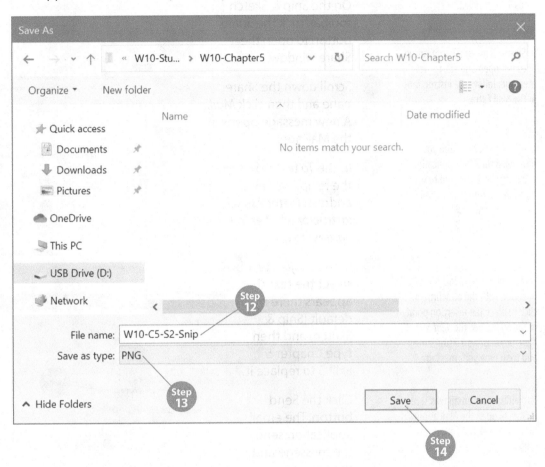

Skill Extra

Annotating Snips

After you capture a snip, you can use the Ballpoint pen tool on the Snip & Sketch toolbar to write on the image by dragging the mouse pointer (or your finger, if you have a touchscreen) over the image; for example, you could circle the most important area of the image.

Beside the Ballpoint pen tool are the Pencil tool and the Highlighter tool. The Highlighter tool works like a real highlighter; drag across an area to highlight it. The Eraser tool erases your pen and highlighter marks.

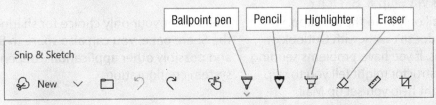

Skill 3
Email an Image Using Snip & Sketch

After capturing a snip, you can use Snip & Sketch to email it to someone via the Mail application that comes with Windows. It does not work with Outlook or other desktop email applications.

TIP

If Snip & Sketch is not still open when you start this skill, repeat Steps 1–9 of Skill 2.

TIP

In Step 2, if an email application does not open and start a new message, follow the instructions in the Skill Extra.

TIP

If Step 3 is the first time you have used the Mail application, you might be prompted to go through a setup process. After it completes, you may have to restart these steps.

TIP

If you would like to include a message with the attachment, click to place the insertion point in the line above the *Sent from Mail for Windows 10* signature and then type your message.

TIP

To confirm your email was sent in Step 6, open the Mail application and check the Sent Items folder.

1. Start with the Snip & Sketch window open and the snip you captured in Skill 2 displayed below the toolbar, and your USB flash drive connected.

2. On the Snip & Sketch toolbar, click the Share button to open the Share window.

3. Scroll down the Share pane and then click *Mail*. A new message opens in the Mail app.

4. In the *To* text box, type the recipient's email address. **Note:** *Ask your instructor what email address to use.*

5. In the *Subject* text box, select the text that appears there by default (Snip & Sketch) and then type Chapter 5 Skill 3 to replace it.

6. Click the Send button. The email application sends the message and then closes.

7. Close all open windows and disconnect your USB flash drive.

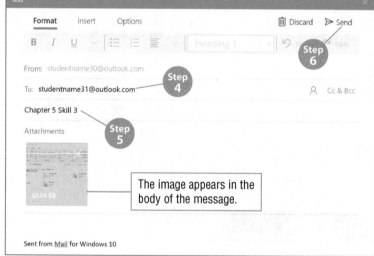

The image appears in the body of the message.

Skill Extra

Trouble Sending Email via Snip & Sketch?

Snip & Sketch sends email only from the Mail app, which comes with Windows; it doesn't work with Outlook or other desktop email apps. If you have problems sending email in this skill, your instructor might tell you to skip sending the email or might help you set up Mail.

Email is not your only choice for sharing. As you saw in the Share pane, you can also share to Skype, OneNote, and possibly other applications, depending on your system configuration.

Skill 4
Create a Notebook, Sections, and Pages in OneNote

OneNote is an application for organizing notes and data, such as research for a school paper or a work project. You can include website content, documents, pictures, and more. The most basic organizing unit of OneNote is a *notebook*. Within a notebook, you can have *sections*, which are like dividers. Each section can have one or more *pages*. In this skill, you will create a

notebook, two sections, and two pages. There are three versions of OneNote: the desktop version, the OneNote app included with Windows 10, and the free online version that is part of the Office for the web suite. In this chapter, you will work with the Windows 10 version of OneNote.

TIP

If both *OneNote App* and *OneNote for Windows 10 App* appear in the search results in Step 2, click *OneNote for Windows 10 App*. The one that's just plain OneNote App is the Microsoft 365 version, not covered in this skill.

1. Click in the search box and then type onenote.

2. When *OneNote for Windows 10 App* appears at the top of the menu, click it to open the OneNote for Windows 10 application.

3. The first time you start OneNote, you might see introductory messages. Respond to these as needed to clear them. For example, there might be a prompt telling you to click to get started taking notes.

4. Click the Show Navigation button to expand the Navigation pane if needed.

5. Click the down arrow to the right of the current notebook name to open a pane.

(6) At the bottom of the pane, click *+ Add notebook*.

(7) Type W10-C5-Notebook in the New Notebook dialog box.

(8) Click the Create Notebook button.

(9) With the insertion point in the title placeholder at the top of the right pane, just above the date, type Page 1 and then press Enter.

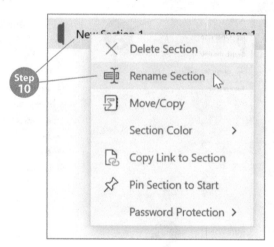

(10) Right-click *New Section 1* in the Sections pane and then click *Rename Section*. The section name becomes editable.

(11) Type Content and then press Enter.

Skill Extra

Working with Other Notebooks

If you already have OneNote notebooks in your OneDrive account, you can access them in this version of OneNote. Click the arrow to the right of the notebook name, and on the menu that appears, click *More Notebooks* to open the Choose notebooks to open dialog box. Select a notebook from the list and then click the Open button.

12 At the bottom of the Page pane, click + *Add page*. An untitled page appears.

13 Right-click *Untitled page* and click *Rename Page*.

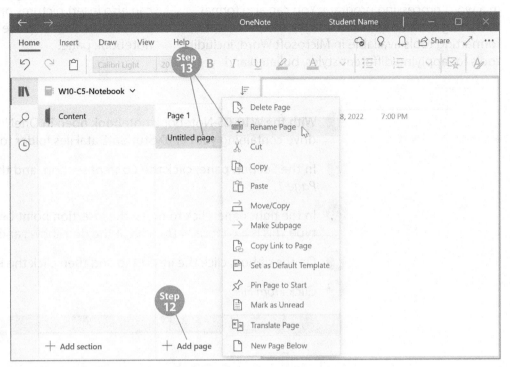

14 In the title placeholder of the new page, type Page 2 and then press Enter.

15 Click + *Add section* at the bottom of the Section pane. A new section appears called *New Section 1* in the Section pane.

16 With the *New Section 1* placeholder name selected, type Miscellaneous and then press Enter. Leave OneNote open for the next skill.

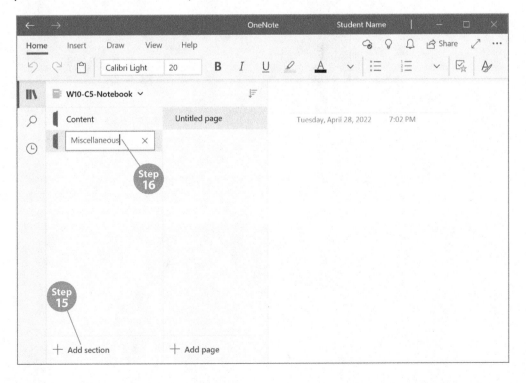

Skill 5

Add Content to a Page in OneNote

Within a OneNote page, you can type text directly, like in a word processing program. You can also format text using the same basic character and paragraph formatting tools available in Microsoft Word, including tools for applying different styles, bulleted and numbered lists, fonts, font sizes, and font colors. You can also insert pictures on a notebook page. In this skill, you will see how to place both text and a picture on a notebook page.

You created the notebook
W10-C5-Notebook in Skill 4.

1 With the W10-C5-Notebook notebook open in OneNote, connect the USB flash drive containing your W10-StudentDataFiles folder to your PC.

2 In the Section pane, click the *Content* section, and then in the Page pane, click *Page 1*.

3 In the right pane, click to move the insertion point below the page title if needed, type This is a picture of Duncan at the dog show., and then press Enter two times.

4 On the ribbon, click the Insert tab and then click the Pictures button.

5 Click *From File*.

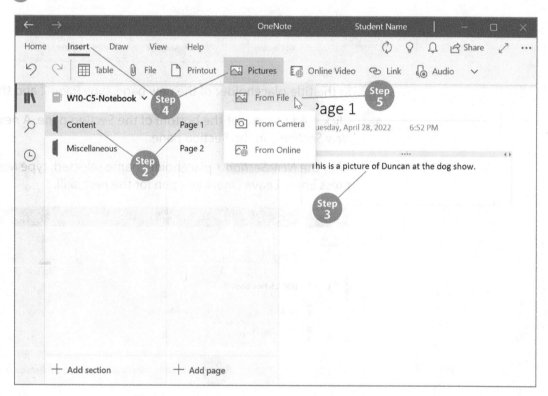

6 In the Open dialog box, navigate to the W10-Chapter5 folder on your USB flash drive.

7 Click the *W10-C5-Duncan* file to select it.

8 Click the Open button to insert the picture on the notebook page at the insertion point position.

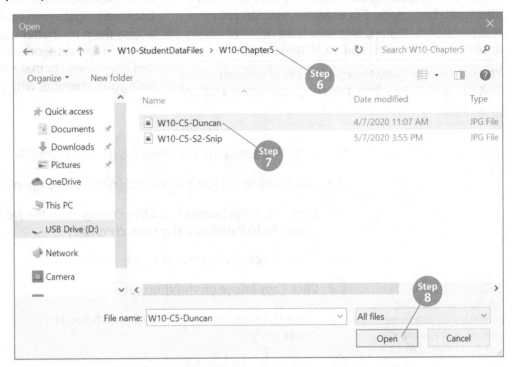

9 Click the picture to select it if needed. Then drag the lower right corner selection handle on the picture (the small white square) inward toward the center of the picture to make it smaller until the right edge of the photo lines up with the end of the word *Duncan*.

10 Click in the text above the picture to deselect the picture. Leave OneNote open to this page for the next skill. Disconnect your USB flash drive.

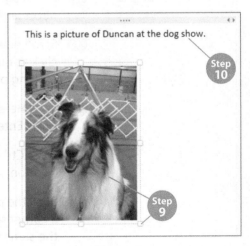

This is a picture of Duncan at the dog show.

Skill Extras

Printing a OneNote Notebook Page

To print a OneNote notebook page, start by clicking the Settings and More (…) button in the upper right corner of the OneNote window. On the menu that appears, click *Print*. In the Print dialog box, use options to specify settings such as the desired printer, number of copies, orientation (portrait or landscape), and color mode. (The options will vary depending on the printer or printers available to your PC.) After making all your selections, click the Print button.

Tagging Content in OneNote

On the Home tab of the OneNote ribbon, clicking the arrow to the right of the Tag this Note button (looks like a check box) opens a menu of tags, which are like categories. You can tag a piece of content to assign a category to it, such as Question, Definition, or To Do item.

Skill 6
Collect and Organize Online Content in OneNote

OneNote works with the Windows Clipboard, which means that you can paste almost any type of content into a notebook page. For example, you can copy and paste text, images, and links from other Windows applications, websites, and email messages.

You can use OneNote to organize lists of web addresses. This can be helpful when gathering sources for a school research paper or a workplace project. Saving web addresses in OneNote has advantages over simply bookmarking them in your web browser. It allows you to access them no matter which browser you are using, and to group and categorize the links for easier retrieval. You can also choose to make text notes about each link to help you remember why you saved it.

Insert a Picture from a Web Page in a OneNote Page

1 Make sure the W10-C5-Notebook notebook is open in OneNote.

2 Open the Edge browser and then navigate to the location https://W10.ParadigmEducation.com/Riley.

3 Right-click the photo on the web page.

4 Click *Copy image* on the shortcut menu.

5 Close the browser window and switch back to OneNote.

6 Click *Page 1* to switch to that page if necessary.

7 Scroll down to the bottom of Page 1 if needed, click to place the insertion point below the existing picture, and then press Enter.

8 Type Here is Riley with his blue ribbon. and then press Enter two times.

9 Press Ctrl + V to paste the new picture in this location.

10 Click the picture you just pasted and then drag a corner selection handle to resize it so that it is the same width as the picture above it.

TIP

You may copy pictures from the internet into OneNote for personal use, such as to help you study, so long as you do not repost the image elsewhere on the web.

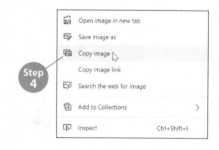

Step 4

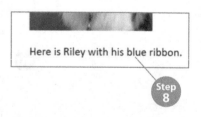

Here is Riley with his blue ribbon.

Step 8

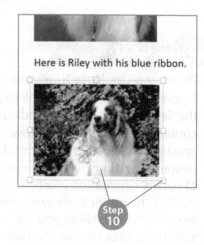

Here is Riley with his blue ribbon.

Step 10

Insert a Link in a OneNote Page

⑪ In the Page pane, click *Page 2* to move to that page.

⑫ If needed, click to move the insertion point below the page title in the right pane.
Type Here's the announcement of Margaret's dog winning his C-ATCH title: https://W10.ParadigmEducation.com/Riley and then press Enter two times.

⑬ On the ribbon, click the Insert tab and then click the Link button. A Link panel opens below the link you just typed.

⑭ Type https://W10.ParadigmEducation.com/CPE in the *Address* box.

⑮ Click in the *Text to display* box and then type CPE Home Page.

⑯ Click the Insert button. The hyperlink appears on the notebook page with the text you specified: <u>CPE Home Page</u>.

TIP

When you type a web address and then press Enter or the Spacebar, OneNote automatically turns the address into a live hyperlink.

TIP

When you click a live hyperlink in a notebook page, OneNote opens the link in a new tab in your browser.

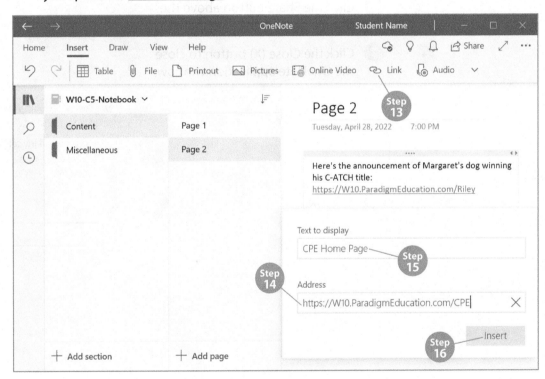

⑰ Leave OneNote open at this page for the next skill.

Skill Extra

Copying and Pasting Web Addresses

Here's a shortcut method for capturing a web page's address in OneNote: Display the desired web page in your web browser, select its address in the Address bar, and then press Ctrl + C to copy the address. In your OneNote notebook page, position the insertion point where you want the address to appear and then press Ctrl + V to paste the link at that location.

Skill 7
Email a Link to OneNote Content

You can send an email containing a link to your OneNote file on your OneDrive, and others can use OneNote to view the notebook. For example, you could place your assignments in a OneNote notebook and then invite your instructor to view it for grading. You can share a OneNote notebook by creating a link to it and sharing the link, or you can send an email directly from OneNote. The recipient can use any available version of OneNote to view your notebook.

TIP

Google Chrome is the preferred web browser for Cirrus. If you have trouble accessing Cirrus with a different browser, switching to Chrome may resolve the problem.

TIP

Ask your instructor what email address to use for the recipient in Step 3.

1. Start with your W10-C5-Notebook file open in OneNote.

2. Click the Share button, which is above the right side of the ribbon.

3. In the Share panel, type the email address of the person you want to invite in the *Send an email invitation* box.

4. Click the Can edit button and then click *Can view*.

5. Click the Share button.

6. Click the Share button above the ribbon to close the Share pane.

7. Click the Close (X) button to close the OneNote application window.

Skill Extra

Emailing a Copy of Your Notebook

Another way to share a notebook is to send a copy of a certain page of content via email to someone. At the bottom of the Share panel, click *Send a copy*. Then in the Share panel that appears, click *Mail*. This doesn't send the actual data file; it sends the content of the active page in the body of the email.

Tasks Summary

Task	Button/Icon/Option	Action
capture a window with Snip & Sketch app		On toolbar, click New button arrow, click *Snip Now*, click Window Snip button, point to window, click window.
create and name OneNote notebook	+ Add notebook	In OneNote, click arrow on current notebook's name, click + *Add notebook*, type notebook name, click *Create Notebook*.
create and name notebook page in OneNote	+ Add page	Click + *Add page*, type page title, press Enter.
create and name notebook section in OneNote	+ Add section	Click + *Add section*, type section title, press Enter.
email image from Snip & Sketch		On toolbar, click Share button. Click *Mail*. In email window, fill in *To* and *Subject* boxes, click Send button.
email a page from OneNote	Share	Above ribbon, click *Share*, click *Send a copy*, and click *Mail*. In *To* box, type email address, click *Send*.
enter text in notebook page in OneNote		Click in desired location below title, type text.
insert online content link in notebook page in OneNote	Link	Click desired position. On ribbon, click Insert tab, click Link button. In *Text to display* box, type link text. In *Address* box, type web page address. Click Insert button.
insert picture in notebook page in OneNote	Pictures	Click desired position. On ribbon, click Insert tab, click *Pictures* click *From File*. In Open dialog box, navigate to folder, click picture file, click Open button.
navigate to a page in OneNote		Click desired section in pane, and then click desired page in Page pane.
save and name screenshot in Snip & Sketch		On toolbar, click Save as button. In Save As dialog box, navigate to folder, type name in *File name* text box, click Save button.
start Snip & Sketch	**Snip** & **Sketch** App	On Windows taskbar, type snip in search box, click *Snip & Sketch App*.
type online content link in notebook in OneNote		On the desired page, click in desired location below title, type web address, press Spacebar or Enter.
view screenshots taken with Windows logo key + Print Screen key	Screenshots	In File Explorer, double-click *Pictures* folder, double-click *Screenshots* folder.

Chapter 6

The online course includes additional training and assessment resources.

Customizing and Maintaining Windows

Windows 10 is very customizable. You can adjust the way input devices like a keyboard and mouse work, what colors the display uses, how loud the volume is when playing sounds and music, and much more. You can also adjust technical settings such as how the computer interacts with networks and how often it runs certain maintenance processes.

There are two main utilities for adjusting settings in Windows 10: the Control Panel and the Settings app. This chapter explains how to work with both, as well as how to adjust sound and display settings, how to connect to wireless networks, and how to make sure the computer's security, maintenance, and update settings are configured correctly.

If your computer is part of a network at school or at work, there may be IT professionals who manage your PC's settings, and your user account might be restricted from making certain system changes or using certain maintenance utilities. If you run into problems reviewing and changing system settings covered in this chapter, make sure that you have the needed permissions before assuming Windows is malfunctioning.

Skills You Learn

1 Explore the Control Panel and the Settings App

2 Personalize the Desktop

3 Modify Screen Brightness and Resolution

4 Adjust the Sound Volume

5 Connect to and Disconnect from a Wireless Network

6 Review Security, Maintenance, and Update Settings

Files You Use

For these skills, you do not need any student data files.

Skill 1
Explore the Control Panel and the Settings App

The *Control Panel* and the *Settings app* are the two main areas of Windows 10 for adjusting settings and performing maintenance. Some settings appear in both places, while other settings are in only one or the other. Microsoft has been gradually moving settings out of the Control Panel and into the Settings app through Windows 10 updates, and eventually the Control Panel will be phased out completely. Until that happens, there are still many settings that require Control Panel access to adjust. This skill illustrates how both utilities work.

Explore the Control Panel

1 Click in the search box on the taskbar, type control, and then click *Control Panel App* in the search results.

TIP

By default, the Control Panel appears in Category view, which organizes the available settings into categories.

TIP

You may see different items in the search results than shown here.

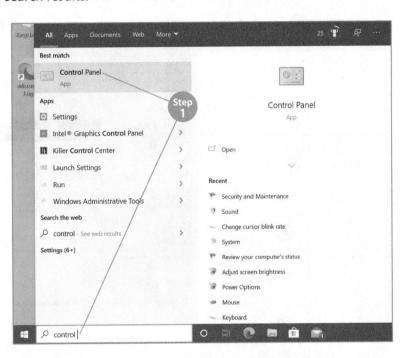

TIP

Large icons view allows you to browse an alphabetical list of settings, which is useful if you don't know which category the desired setting is in.

2 Click the *View by* box arrow and then click *Large icons* in the drop-down list.

3 Click the *View by* box arrow again and then click *Category* to return to the default view.

4 Click <u>System and Security</u> to display the settings in that category.

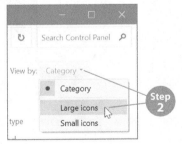

5 Click <u>System</u> to display basic information about your computer.

6 In the Address bar, click *Control Panel* to return to the top level of the Control Panel.

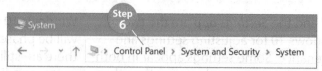

7 Click in the Control Panel search box and then type keyboard to display a list of settings you can change for the keyboard.

8 Click <u>Change cursor blink rate</u> to open the Keyboard Properties dialog box.

9 Drag the *Cursor blink rate* slider to a moderate setting between *None* and *Fast*, if it is not already set that way.

10 Click the OK button to close the Keyboard Properties dialog box.

11 Click the Close (X) button to close the Control Panel app window.

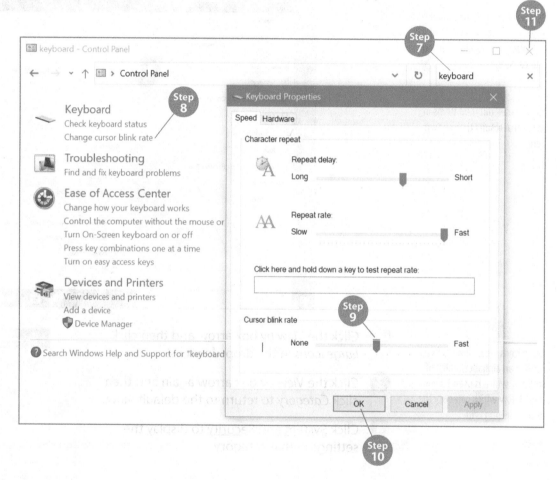

Responding to User Account Control (UAC) Prompts When Changing Settings

Some of the settings you can change require you to be signed in with an administrator account. This type of account is authorized to make changes that affect the entire system, not just one user's settings. In the Control Panel, such settings are identified by a small shield icon (🛡). If you are signed in with a standard (regular) account when you attempt to access such settings, you will be prompted to type the password for an administrator account.

Explore the Settings App

12-13 *Another Way*
Click in the search box on the Windows taskbar, type settings, and then click *Settings App* in the search results list. You can also press Windows logo key + I to open the Settings app.

TIP

In Step 15, if you do not see the Navigation pane, widen the Settings window.

12 Click the Start button.

13 Click *Settings*.

14 Click *System*.

15 In the Navigation pane, scroll down to the bottom and click *About* to display basic information about your computer.

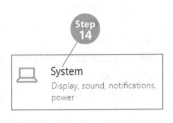

16 Click the Back arrow to return to the main screen of the Settings app.

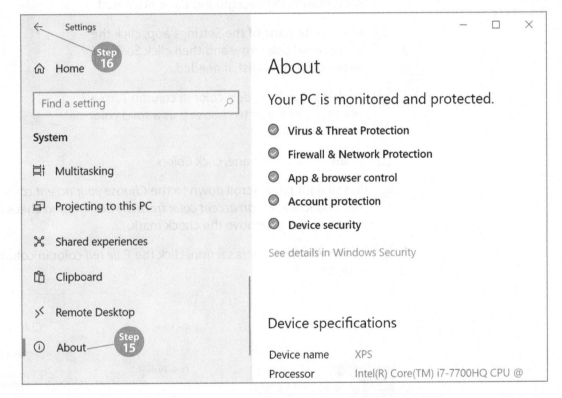

17 Click in the *Find a setting* box and then type mouse to display a list of mouse settings.

18 Click *Mouse settings* in the search results list.

19 Examine the mouse settings available.

20 Click the Close (X) button on the Settings window to close the Settings app.

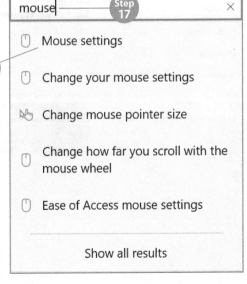

TIP

The mouse settings you can adjust in the Settings app are basic; many more options are available in the Control Panel. You can click *Additional mouse options* after Step 18 to open the Mouse Properties dialog box with all the options in one place.

Skill 2
Personalize the Desktop

You can change a variety of appearance settings to make your desktop reflect your personal preferences. For example, you can choose a photo to appear as the background or change the color of the Title bars and borders on the windows. You can save your settings as a theme and switch between themes whenever you like. A *theme* is a stored collection of settings that include the background image, window color, sound effects, and mouse pointer. (See the Skill Extra section to learn more about system sounds and mouse pointers.)

1 *Another Way*
Instead of completing Step 1, you can click the Start button, click *Settings*, and then click *Personalization*.

1 Right-click a blank area of the desktop and then click *Personalize* on the shortcut menu. This opens the Settings app to the *Personalization* section with the Background page displayed.

2 In the right pane of the Settings app, click the *Background* box arrow and then click *Solid color* in the drop-down list, if needed.

3 Click the *Purple shadow* color in column 7, row 2 of the color palette to choose it as a solid color for the background.

4 In the Navigation pane, click *Colors*.

5 In the right pane, scroll down to the *Choose your accent color* section. If the *Automatically pick an accent color from my background* check box contains a check mark, click it to remove the check mark.

6 In the *Windows colors* section, click the *Pale red* color in column 1, row 2 of the palette.

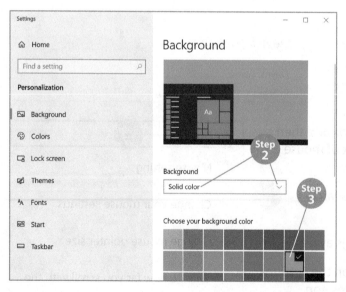

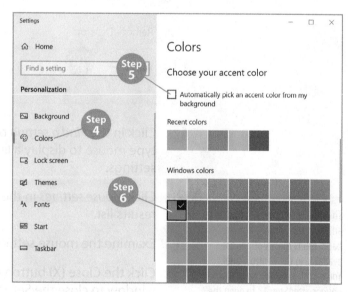

7 Scroll down below the color swatches and click the *Start, taskbar, and action center* check box to insert a check mark, if necessary. The color you chose in Step 6 is applied to the Start menu, Windows taskbar buttons, and Action Center.

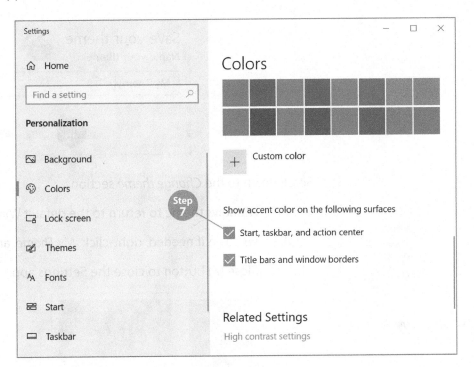

8 Click the *Start, taskbar, and action center* check box again to remove the check mark.

9 In the Navigation pane, click *Themes*.

10 In the right pane, scroll down if needed and then click the Save theme button.

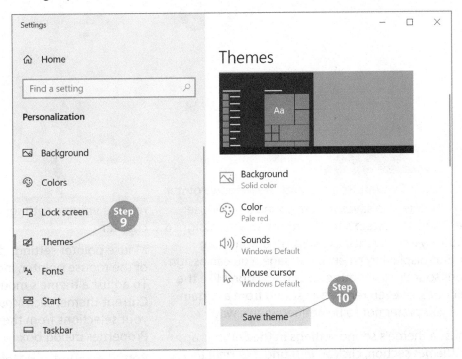

11 In the *Name your theme* box, type My Theme.

12 Click the Save button.

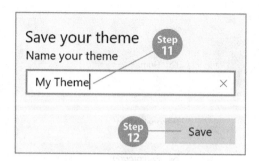

13 Scroll down to the *Change theme* section.

14 Click the *Windows* theme to return to the default Windows theme settings.

15 Scroll down again if needed, right-click *My Theme*, and then click *Delete*.

16 Click the Close (X) button to close the Settings app.

TIP

If your school uses a different theme as its default, choose that in Step 14. Check with your instructor if you have questions.

TIP

If you don't see *My Theme* in Step 15, scroll down.

TIP

If you don't see *Delete* in Step 15, repeat Step 14. You cannot delete the active theme, and you cannot delete any of the built-in themes.

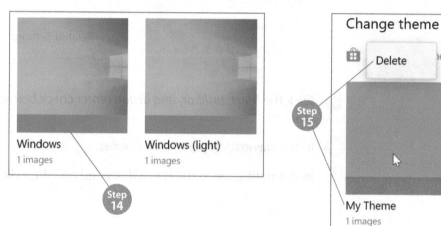

Skill Extra

Personalizing System Sounds and the Mouse Pointer

Saving a theme also saves system sound and mouse pointer choices. *System sounds* are the sounds assigned to various system events, like starting up, shutting down, and displaying an error message. You can assign different sounds to various events if you don't like the default ones, or even remove all sound from a certain event if you prefer not to be notified in this way.

To adjust a theme's sound settings in the Settings app, in the *Themes* section, click *Sounds* under *Current theme*, and then make your selections from the Sounds tab of the Sound dialog box. Overall volume settings and

relative volume settings are explored in Skill 4 of this chapter.

Mouse pointer settings determine the appearance of the mouse pointer, including its size and color. To adjust a theme's mouse pointer settings, under Current theme, click *Mouse cursor*, and then make your selections from the Pointers tab of the Mouse Properties dialog box.

Both the Sound and Mouse Properties dialog boxes can also be accessed directly from the Control Panel.

Skill 3
Modify Screen Brightness and Resolution

Display *brightness* is the amount of light that the screen generates. Most monitors look best at maximum brightness. However, a brighter image uses more power, so if battery life is an issue, you might choose to run at less than maximum brightness to save power. Windows can manage the brightness level automatically if you allow it to do so, dimming the display when running on battery power and brightening it again when running on AC power.

Screen resolution is the number of *pixels* (individually colored dots) vertically and horizontally that make up the display. It is usually described as two numbers, like this: 1920 x 1080. The first number is the number

of pixels horizontally, and the second number is the number of pixels vertically.

The higher the resolution, the smaller text and icons will appear in Windows, and the sharper and crisper the screen will look. When Windows installs, it automatically sets itself up for the highest resolution that the display adapter and monitor support. If you run Windows in a lower resolution than the monitor's maximum, the screen image might look fuzzy. For this reason, most people prefer to run Windows in their monitor's maximum resolution. However, your instructor might ask you to set the resolution in a specific way for an individual assignment or project.

1. Right-click a blank area of the desktop and then click *Display settings* to open the Settings app to the *System* section with the Display page active.

TIP

The *Change brightness* slider is available only on a computer with a built-in display. If you do not see this control in Step 2, you can use brightness controls on the monitor itself.

2. Drag the *Change brightness for the built-in display* slider all the way to the right, to the brightest level (100).

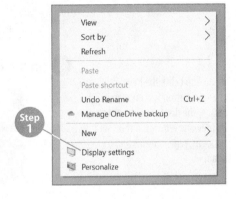

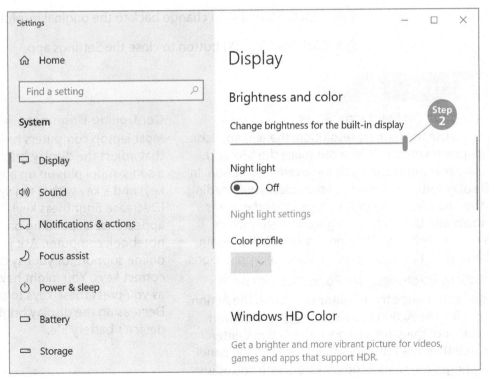

TIP

In Step 3, if you don't see the *Display resolution* box, scroll down.

TIP

The list of available screen resolutions varies depending on the monitor and the graphics adapter.

3 Scroll down to the *Scale and layout* section, click the *Display resolution* box arrow, note the current setting, and then click a different screen resolution in the drop-down list.

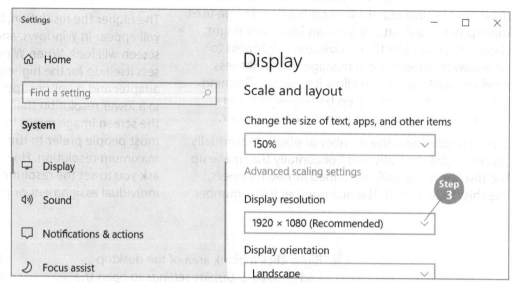

TIP

If you don't click the Keep changes button fast enough in Step 4, the display will revert to its previous settings. If this happens, repeat Step 3 and try again.

4 In the confirmation box, click the Keep changes button.

5 Repeat Steps 3–4 to change back to the original resolution.

6 Click the Close (X) button to close the Settings app.

Skill Extras

Changing the Text and Icon Sizes

When you use the highest resolution, the text and icons might appear very small. You can make the text and icons larger without changing the overall resolution. In the Display settings under the *Scale and layout* heading, click the *Change the size of text, apps, and other items* box arrow and then select a higher setting (such as *125%*). You might need to sign out and back in again for the new setting to take effect across all applications.

Controlling Brightness for Power Management

You can also change the brightness through the Action Center. Click the Action Center icon (▢) in the lower right corner of the screen to open the Action Center panel and then drag the Brightness slider on the panel. This setting is only for laptops; on a desktop you adjust the display brightness on the monitor itself.

Controlling Brightness with the Keyboard

Most laptop computers have buttons on the keyboard that adjust the display brightness. Look for a key with a sun symbol plus an up arrow (Increase Brightness key) and a key with a sun symbol plus a down arrow (Decrease Brightness key). The symbols may vary in appearance depending on the brand and age of the notebook computer. Ask your instructor for help or get online support for your system if needed to identify the correct keys. You might have to hold down the Fn key as you press these keys to adjust the brightness level. Decreasing the display brightness can help extend the device's battery life.

Skill 4
Adjust the Sound Volume

Most computers have sound support, which allows you to hear sounds when system events occur like starting up and shutting down. Sound support also enables you to play music on your PC.

Windows includes a volume control in the notification area of the Windows taskbar, providing a quick shortcut for adjusting the overall volume of sounds on the PC. You can also adjust the volumes individually for different kinds of sounds. For example, you might make the volume for your music player application louder than the volume for system sounds. You can also mute the sound entirely.

TIP

The name of the icon you click in Step 1 might be different, depending on your computer's hardware. For example, the name might be Speakers/Headphones on a laptop that has only one jack for both.

1. In the notification area of the Windows taskbar, click the speaker icon to display the volume control box.

2. Drag the slider to adjust the volume to level 56.

3. Click the Mute button to turn off all sounds.

4. Click the Mute button to turn on all sounds.

5. Click any blank area of the desktop to close the volume control box.

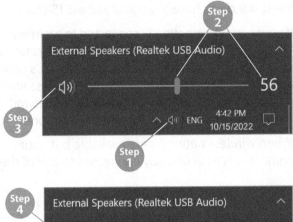

Skill Extras

Adjusting the Recording Volume

If your computer has a microphone or other audio input device, you can control its volume. In the notification area of the Windows taskbar, right-click the speaker icon and then click *Open Sound settings* to open the *Sound* section of the Settings app. Scroll down if needed to the *Input* section. Click the *Choose your input device* box arrow and click the desired recording device (for example, *Microphone*) and then click Device properties to open its Properties box. Set its volume by dragging the Volume slider. Close the Settings app when finished.

Troubleshooting Sound Problems

If the sound isn't playing as expected on your computer, right-click the Speakers icon in the notification area of the Windows taskbar and then click *Troubleshoot sound problems*. In the Get Help window that appears, type a description of the problem you are having. You must be online for this to work.

Adjusting the Relative Volumes of Different Applications

You can use the Sound Mixer to control the volume for an individual application or output device. In the notification area of the Windows taskbar, right-click the Speakers icon and then click *Open Volume mixer*. Individual sliders and Mute/Unmute buttons appear for your speakers or headphones, system sounds, and other active sound-producing applications or devices. For example, if Windows Media Player or Skype is open, there will be a separate slider and Mute/Unmute button for it.

Connect to and Disconnect from a Wireless Network

If you use a computer that has wireless networking capability, you might use it to connect to a Wi-Fi hotspot. A *hotspot* is a wireless router, which is a connection box that can communicate with wireless-enabled devices via radio frequency (RF) waves. *Wi-Fi* is the informal nickname for the standard that almost all hotspots use; its technical name is *IEEE 802.11*. Wi-Fi hotspots using the latest standards have a range of at least 150 feet.

If your computer is already connected to a wireless network, a Wireless icon appears in the notification area of the Windows taskbar, like this: 📶. Your PC's network adapter can be connected to only one wireless network at a time, so when you connect to a different network, you automatically disconnect from the previous one.

When wireless networks are available but your computer is not currently connected to any of them,

the Wireless icon appears in the notification area as a globe, like this: 🌐. You can choose to have your computer connect to a particular Wi-Fi hotspot whenever it is within range, so you don't have to go through the connection process every time you want to connect.

A *secure router* is one that has some sort of password protection on it. A *security key* is like a password for the router. Security keys are the standard way of connecting to a secure router. If you are connecting to a secure router in your workplace, at school, or in a public place, you will probably use a security key. A *PIN* (personal identification number) is an alternative to a security key, and is an option mainly on small routers sold for personal home use.

Note: *You will need a computer with wireless capability and access to a wireless network to complete this skill.*

> **TIP**
> The networks you see will be different from the ones shown in this skill.

> **TIP**
> In Step 2, if only one network is listed and you are already connected to it, click it, click the Disconnect button, and then click the network again to select it.

1 In the notification area of the Windows taskbar, click the Wireless icon to display a pane listing the available networks.

2 Click the desired network (*Sycamore5* in the example shown).

3 **Optional:** Click the *Connect automatically* check box to insert a check mark if you want your PC to connect to this network automatically in the future.

4 Click the Connect button.

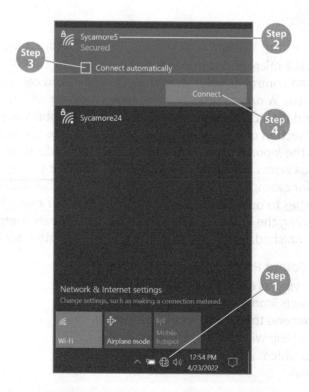

5 If prompted to enter a security key, complete the appropriate step below. *Note: Check with your instructor if you need help.*

5a To connect using a PIN, type the 8-digit PIN printed on your router's label and then click the Next button.

5b To connect using a security key, type the network security key and then click the Next button.

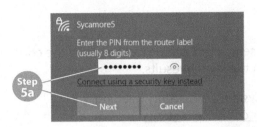 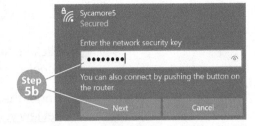

6 If this is the first time you have connected to this network, a prompt might appear asking if you want to find content automatically on the network. Choose one of two options:

6a If this is a home or work network, click the Yes button to turn on file sharing so you can exchange files with other users.

6b If this is a school or public network, click the No button to disable file sharing so others will not be able to browse your files.

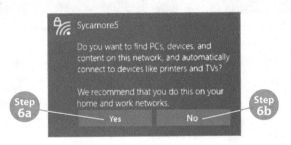 

7 Click outside the wireless pane to close it.

8 In the notification area of the Windows taskbar, click the Wireless icon.

9 Click the network that shows *Connected* under its name.

10 Click the Disconnect button.

11 Click outside the wireless pane to close it.

5a Another Way
Routers that support PINs also support security keys. When prompted to enter a PIN, if you prefer, you can click Connect using a security key instead and follow the instructions in Step 5b.

TIP
Some routers support a feature called Wi-Fi Protected Access (WPA). You can press the WPA button on the router to allow nearby devices to connect with it without a security key or PIN. The permission times out after a minute or two, so you must act quickly after pressing the WPA button to use this method. Consult your router's documentation for more details.

Skill Extra

Using Airplane Mode
Airplane mode temporarily disables your Wi-Fi hardware so that it doesn't search for or connect to a wireless network. To use it, click the Wireless icon in the notification area of the Windows taskbar and then click *Airplane mode*. To return to regular functionality, click the Wireless icon again (which looks like an airplane now) and then click *Airplane mode*. Airplane mode, as the name implies, is useful when you are using your computer in an environment where Wi-Fi usage is not permitted, such as on an airplane during takeoff and landing.

Skill 6

Review Security, Maintenance, and Update Settings

Windows 10 is mostly self-maintaining. The correct settings are enabled automatically to ensure trouble-free operation for most users. The *Security and Maintenance* section of the Control Panel summarizes the status of important security and maintenance areas and lets you know if any action is recommended. The *Windows Update* section of the Settings app allows you to check for Windows updates.

1 Click in the search box on the taskbar and type control. Click *Control Panel App* in the search results.

TIP

You may need special permission to open some of the security features described in this skill.

2 Under the *System and Security* heading, click <u>Review your computer's status</u>.

TIP

Messages with a red bar are important problems to be addressed. Messages with a yellow bar are warnings and might not need action.

3 Under the *Security* heading, review any messages with a red or yellow bar and take the appropriate action. **Note:** *Ask your instructor if you are unsure what to do about a message.*

4 Click the *Security* heading down arrow to display more security settings, if needed.

TIP

If you see the message "No issues have been detected by Security and Maintenance," you have no issues to address.

5 Scroll through the list of security settings to review their status.

TIP

You might see warning messages above the Security heading. None are shown here.

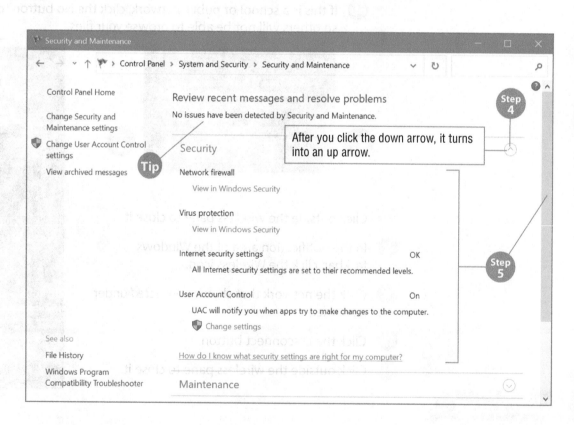

System and Security
Review your computer's status
Save backup copies of your files with File History
Backup and Restore (Windows 7)

Step 2

Security and Maintenance

Control Panel > System and Security > Security and Maintenance

Control Panel Home
Change Security and Maintenance settings
Change User Account Control settings
View archived messages

Review recent messages and resolve problems
No issues have been detected by Security and Maintenance.

Security

Network firewall
View in Windows Security

Virus protection
View in Windows Security

Internet security settings   OK
All Internet security settings are set to their recommended levels.

User Account Control   On
UAC will notify you when apps try to make changes to the computer.
Change settings

See also
File History
Windows Program Compatibility Troubleshooter

Maintenance

How do I know what security settings are right for my computer?

Step 4

After you click the down arrow, it turns into an up arrow.

Step 5

6 Click the *Security* heading up arrow to collapse the section.

7 Click the *Maintenance* heading down arrow to review maintenance settings.

8 Scroll through the list of maintenance settings to review their status. For example, note the last run date in the *Automatic Maintenance* section.

9 Click the Close (X) button to close the window.

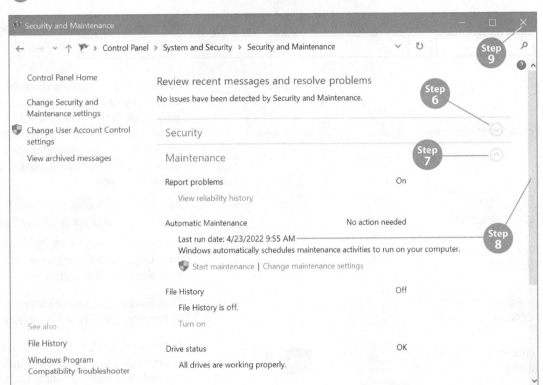

TIP

Settings that have a <u>Change settings</u> link can be modified by clicking that option. If there is a shield symbol next to the option, making changes requires administrator permission.

10 Click the Start button and then click *Settings*. Click *Home*, if needed, to return to the Home screen.

TIP

In Step 11, you might need to scroll down to see the Update & Security button.

11 Click *Update & Security* to open the *Windows Update* section.

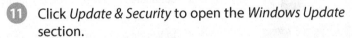

Update & Security
Windows Update, recovery, backup

12 Click the Check for updates button if it appears, and wait for the check to complete. If any updates are found, they are usually downloaded and installed automatically. You might see a notice that a restart has been scheduled for installing updates. If a major update is available, you might have to click a Download or Install button to accept it.

TIP

In Step 13, you can close the Settings app while the updates are being downloaded and installed; the process will continue. The Settings app might close automatically.

13 Click the Close (X) button to close the Settings app.

Skill Extra

Updating Other Microsoft Products

If you have Microsoft Office or other Microsoft applications installed, your computer can automatically receive updates for them. In the *Windows Update* section of the Settings app, you can click *Advanced options* and then drag the *Receive updates for other Microsoft products when you update Windows* toggle to the *On* or *Off* position.

Tasks Summary

Task	Button/Icon/Option	Action
adjust sound volume	External Speakers (Realtek USB Audio) ⊲× ——●—— 26	In Windows taskbar notification area, click speaker icon, drag slider, click away to close slider.
apply default theme	Windows 1 images	In *Personalization* section of Settings app, on Themes page, under *Change theme* heading, click *Windows*.
change desktop colors	☒ Background	In Navigation pane of *Personalization* section of Settings app, click *Background*, click *Background* box arrow, click *Solid color*, click desired color swatch. In Navigation pane, click *Colors*, remove check mark from *Automatically pick an accent color from my background* check box if needed, click desired color swatch, insert check mark in *Start, taskbar, and action center* check box.
change screen brightness (laptop)	Change brightness for the built-in display ————————●—	At desktop, right-click any blank area, click *Display settings*, drag *Change brightness for the built-in display* slider.
change screen resolution	Display resolution 1920 × 1080 (Recommended) ∨	At desktop, right-click any blank area, click *Display settings*, click *Display resolution* box arrow, click desired resolution, click Keep Changes button.
check for Windows Updates	↻ Update & Security Windows Update, recovery, backup	Click Start button, click *Settings*. At Settings app, click *Update & Security*, click Check for updates button.
connect to a wireless network	🌐	In Windows taskbar notification area, click Wireless icon, click desired network, click Connect button, type PIN or security key and click *Next* if prompted to do so.
delete theme	Delete	In *Personalization* section of the Settings app, under *Themes*, right-click theme, click *Delete*.
disconnect from a wireless network	📶	In Windows taskbar notification area, click Wireless icon, click connected network, click Disconnect button, click outside pane to close it.
mute/unmute sound	🔊 🔇	In Windows taskbar notification area, click speaker icon, click the Mute button.
open Control Panel	Control Panel App	Click in search box on taskbar, type control, click *Control Panel app*.
open *Personalization* section of Settings app	Personalize	At desktop, right-click any blank area, click *Personalize*.
open Settings app	⚙	Click Start button, click *Settings*.
review security and maintenance settings	System and Security Review your computer's status	From Control Panel, under *System and Security*, click Review your computer's status.
save new theme after changing desktop colors	☑ Themes	After changing to desired settings, from *Themes* section of Settings app, click Save theme button. In Save your theme dialog box, type name, click Save button.

Glossary and Index

Security and Maintenance section of, 94–95

Sound and Mouse Properties dialog box, 88

User Account Control (UAC) prompts, 84

cookie A small text file placed on a user's hard disk by a web page in order to facilitate communications that require remembering information, such as the contents of a shopping cart or a user's country of residence. 45

blocking, 46

clearing browser history, 45–46

copying and pasting

files using copy and paste, 30–31

files using drag-and-drop, 29–30

files using Move To button on Home tab, 31

group of files from local hard drive to USB flash drive, 16

images using Snip & Sketch, 69–71

moving and copying files using, 30–31

web addresses into OneNote, 79

Cortana button, 68

Cortana Microsoft's user-friendly search tool, capable of responding to English-language voice requests. 48

using voice commands with, 48

creating files, 22–23

in OneDrive, 56

customizing, 82

desktop background and theme colors, 86–87

user icon in OneDrive, 54

D

data file A file that stores data a user has entered using a

computer, such as a word processing document. 29

downloading and extracting student, 24–25

deleted files, 16

restoring, 33

stored in Recycle Bin, 32

deleting

browser history, 45–46

files, 16, 32–33

files from Recycle Bin, 32–33

files in One Drive, 56

folders in Users folder, 20

turning off confirmation box for, 33

deletion confirmation, turning off, 33

desktop application A type of application designed to run on the Windows desktop; prior to Windows 8, this was the only type of application available. *See also* **Modern app**, 6

desktop The background area of the Windows interface. *See also* **desktop application**, 3

creating a new, 10

personalizing, 86–88

working with multiple, 10

dialog box A window that prompts the user to provide additional information about a command or action being taken. 11

using, 12

Disk Cleanup utility, 32

.docx extension, 16

Dogpile, 42

download To transfer a file from the internet to your computer. *See also* **upload**, 57

executable files, 25

file from a website, 43

as opposite of uploading, 57

reducing malware risk, 43

ZIP file, 24–25

drag-and-drop To move or copy an onscreen item to a different location by pointing to it, holding down the left mouse button, moving the mouse, and releasing the left mouse button. 4, 29

file or folder onto an icon, 31

moving and copying files using, 29–30

drop-down list, 12, 13

DuckDuckGo, 42

E

Edge. *See* **Microsoft Edge**, 38

editing

documents in Microsoft 365 applications, 61–63

file in Microsoft web-based app, 60

file on local PC, 52

read-only access and, 64

Edit View, in Microsoft web-based app, 60

Eject Media command, 18

email

address in OneNote, 80

copy of OneNote notebook, 80

downloading executable files from, 25

images using Snip & Sketch, 72

link to OneNote content, 80

Eraser tool, on Snip & Sketch, 71

Error icon, 58

errors, resolving upload, 58

Esc key, 4

Excel, application for Microsoft 365, 61

Excel, application for Microsoft Office for the web, 60, 62

sign in To identify yourself by entering your credentials (user account and password) in Windows and other applications. 2

instructions, 2

sign out To end your Windows session without shutting down the computer. 2

instructions, 2

Skype, 72

Sleep, 2

snapping apps, 8

Snip & Sketch An application that enables users to capture a screenshot of a part of the computer screen. 69

annotating snips, 71

capturing image of entire screen using, 67–68

capturing portion of screen using, 69–71

emailing an image using, 72

Eraser tool, 71

Highlighter tool, 71

Pencil tool, 72

trouble sending email via, 72

Sound Mixer, 91

sound volume, adjusting, 91

speaker icon, 4

Start button The button at the far left end of the Windows taskbar when clicked it opens the Start menu. 2, 3

Start menu A menu of commands and applications a user can access to run programs, manage files, access system setting and utilities, and perform other activities in Windows. 3

main function of, 3

open and close applications from the, 5–6

shortcut appearing as tiles on, 3

storage, data files, 17

student data files

downloading, 24–25

uploading, 51–52

symbols, in file or folder names, 23

sync Short for synchronize; generally refers to updating copies of data files stored in multiple locations so that all copies are the same. 51

choosing which folders to, in OneDrive, 52

controlling with OneDrive, 63

system sounds Sounds that play when certain system events happen in the operating system, such as starting up, shutting down, or an error occurring. 88

T

tabbed browsing, in Microsoft Edge, 40

tagging content in OneNote, 77

Talk to Cortana, 3

taskbar. *See* **Windows taskbar**, 3

Task View button, 3

vertical scroll bar, 10

text

changing size of, 90

formatting, 76

theme A named collection of formatting settings; in Windows, a theme controls the desktop background, window colors, and system sounds. 88

default, 88

sound settings, 88

third-party cookie, 46. *See also* **cookie**

thumbnail image, 4

tile A large, rectangular button on the Start menu, representing an application or location you can access by clicking it. 3

Timeline, 10

toolbar In some applications, a row of graphical buttons, each of which represents a command. 11

Snip & Sketch, 69

using a, 11–12

touchscreen, xiv

dragging on a, 4

troubleshooting

network problems, 14

sound problems, 91

turning off the computer, 2

Twitter, 72

U

uniform resource locator (URL) A unique web address, typically beginning with the protocol *https://www*. 38

manually typing into Address bar, 41

Universal app. *See* **Microsoft Store app**, 3

updates

checking for, 95

Microsoft products, 95

upload To transfer a file from your local PC to an online location. *See also* **download**, 57

dragging to, 58

files and folders to OneDrive, 51

files via File Explorer, 51–52

files via OneDrive, 57–58

resolving errors in, 58

USB flash drive, xi

in Navigation pane, 18

safely disconnecting, 18

user account, 2

making system changes in, 82

picture for, 2

signing in with, 2

user folders and, 17, 20

User Account Control (UAC) prompts, 84

User folders, 20, 22

user name, signing in with, 2

user icon, customizing in OneDrive, 54

V

vertical scroll bar, 10

View options button, 56

Virtual Agent A help feature that enables you to ask questions in natural language, rather than searching by keywords. 14

voice commands, using with Cortana, 48

volume A portion of a physical disk that is assigned a certain letter in a computer's storage system, such as *C:*. A volume can be a USB flash drive, an optical disc such as a DVD, an entire hard disk drive, or a portion of a hard disk drive. 16

  adjusting, 91

  examples, 16

  navigating between folders and local (File Explorer), 17–18

volume name, 17

W

W-10-Backup window, 31

W10-C4-Miscellaneous folder, 64

W10-StudentDataFiles, 50

  uploading student data files, 51

web addresses

  copying and pasting, 79

  live hyperlinks, 79

  saving in OneNote, 78

web An interconnected set of publicly accessible file servers and routers on the internet, storing and serving up web pages. 38

  copying and pasting address in OneNote, 79

searching with the search box on taskbar, 36

web browser An application that enables the user to access web pages. 38.

  navigating in, 39

web page A document or page stored on a web server and available on the web. 38

  printing, 47

  zooming in and out on, 42

web servers, 38

website A collection of related web pages. 38

  downloading a file from, 43

  naming folders and files from, 23

  redirects to other, 40

Wi-Fi. *See also* **IEEE 802.11**, 92

  airplane mode and, 93

Wi-Fi Protected Access (WPA), 93

window A well-defined rectangular area onscreen in which an application runs, a file listing appears, or a message displays. 1, 7

  closing a minimized, 8

  manipulating, 7–8

  minimizing all open, 8

  moving and resizing using keyboard, 8

  moving between open, 9–10

  snapping app and automatically maximize, 8

  states of, 7

Windows Accessories, 5

Windows Fax and Scan app, 11

Windows logo key, 4, 67

Window Snip, 69

Windows Search, 48. *See also* **search box**

  using to get information online, 48

Windows taskbar The Windows taskbar contains the Start

button, a search box, pinned buttons, the notification area, a clock, and a button that opens the Action Center. 3

  closing a minimized window from the, 8

  colored line under a button on, 7

  minimizing all open windows using, 8

  New desktop button from, 10

  searching for files with search box on, 36

  searching for help using, 14

  searching the web with, 36

WinZIP, 28

wireless network, connecting and disconnecting from, 92–93

Word, application for Microsoft 365. *See* Microsoft Word for Microsoft 365, 50, 63

Word, application for Microsoft Office for the web. *See* Microsoft Word web-based app, 59–60

WordPad app, 68

  pasting images into, 67

  using a ribbon, 11

worldwide web. *See* **web**, 38

Y

Yahoo, 42

Z

.zip extension, 16, 24

ZIP file A compressed archive file that holds multiple individual files in a single named file, compressing each file so that it is smaller than it was originally. 24

  creating a, 27–28

  downloading and extracting student data files, 24–25

  running, 24

Zooming, 42